Prologue

'The bricks of this narrative are true, the mortar has been made up.'

Christmas Island
25th March 1958 18th March 1959

John Smart got the nick name 'Sambo' when he went to his primary school. Robinson decided on it. The reason is unclear: John was a particularly pale child in fact so pale that he often got asked if he felt well; he soon learned to say that he felt a bit ill and would either spend time in the secretary's office or, better still, be sent home.

Upon joining the army as a boy soldier the nick name stuck but was shortened to Sam. The theory was that there were too many Johns around, 'say 'John!' they said 'and the crick of necks was deafening!'

Since leaving the army Sam has become a distinctly separate character; sillier or wiser; more or less brave than John. A useful character to have around if you need a story telling.

Christmas Island is in the middle of the Pacific Ocean as near as makes no difference.

During Sam's stay on the island there were four and a half thousand men stationed there. Mostly army and air force with a smaller group of Royal Navy. There were also two women, WVS ladies who provided a motherly influence to any who could not take the strain.

The exercise was Operation Grapple, its purpose the development of Britain's nuclear deterrent. The world was a dangerous place then. William Penny was the chief scientist.

CHAPTER 1

Brompton Barracks

Mistakes

Sam Smart often made mistakes in planning his life. Not from any wicked intention; most of his mistakes came about as the result of trying to make himself comfortable. Sam liked his life to be comfortable; free from decision, free from discomfort, free from rush and hurry. Staying away from school was one such mistake. A fairly small decision from Sam's point of view, it had provided the comfort of doing what he wanted to do when he wanted to do it rather than having to be in class so and so at such and such a time. It was a mistake that had resulted in him being persuaded, in no uncertain terms by his Father, to join the army. Thus it had resulted in no comfort and no freedom. None at all.

Five years later we find him busy making another mistake...

'Put a one before the nine and we've added ten days! No first parade for another week at least'. Sam amended the chit to show nineteen days excused parade.

'Brilliant mate,' Scouse Smith grinned and lit a cigarette.'

'Oi!, you can't smoke in here. Put it out. The orderly behind the desk in the hospital out patients department pointed his pencil at Scouse as if it was a weapon. The Liverpudlean nipped the burning tip from the ciggy and put the unsmoked remainder behind his ear.

It had been Sam's idea, another fairly small decision - again from Sam's point of view - but one destined to alter the uneven path of his life in a big way. Getting out of the cold and joyless ritual of first parade each morning at seven thirty was a goal worth achieving.

Brompton Barracks School of Military Engineering was,

Sam reckoned, a Victorian institution. A triumphant stone arch almost the size of Marble Arch led one onto a vast parade square of yellow gravel that lay between the pale grey buildings. This square was only for parading on. To venture onto it casually was an act of blasphemy in the view of the Beast - the provost sergeant who lurked in the guard room to the left. The Beast was short and stocky with wild bushy eyebrows arching over wild burning eyes. He had a low and menacing voice that carried to the most distant corners of the barracks and yet, curiously it did not seem loud. Almost more of a presence than a sound. Sam thought it would have sounded much like God did to Moses.

The grey buildings surrounding the square were, again in Sam's opinion, typically Victorian. With a basement, a ground and a first floor. Sam and Scouse were housed in the basement along with the rest of the course gathered to learn about pumps and refrigeration mechanics. Some thirty men in all. The billet lay to the right of the square and was cold, with whitewashed walls and bars at the windows. It was ancient dry, like a newly opened tomb and smelled of dust winter and summer alike. The theory was that horses had been stabled here

'In its hay day!' Scouse had remarked, ever the wit.

The officers quarters lay at the opposite end of the square to the 'Marble Arch' and housed many treasures acquired during campaigns in which the Royal Engineers had made their mark. The whole barracks was angular, ornate and grand; designed to intimidate the likes of Sam Smart and Scouse Smith. To overcome it in some small way was very worth ones while.

The ruse

Both had come down with a cold - it was late October - reported sick and made sufficient fuss about dizziness and blocked sinuses to persuade the medical officer that excused duties or hospital treatment would do the trick. The MO, a grizzled old Captain nearing the end of his service, thought that once these two skiving hounds had suffered a bit of sinus pumping they would beg for the treatment to end and be 'cured' in two days. He signed the chit giving them two days treatment at the local hospital; until the ninth of November, nineteen fifty seven. Being old school the captain always wrote the date, 'properly', in full. None of this oh nine nonsense, '9th' he wrote on both their chits. So Sam had devised the idea of putting the one in front thus giving them until the nineteenth of November with no parade.

Once the two days treatment was finished - they had both suffered having their heads blown up! - on day three, they had gone straight to the Cosy Cafe at the top of Brompton high street setting a pattern that they hoped to follow for the remaining days allowed on the chit. Here they could smoke and drink tea for an hour or so before reporting for duty at the workshops where they continued to learn the nuances of centrifugal pumps etc.

As Sam had misjudged his Father's abilities to spot the wrong behaviour in a boy supposedly not happy at school, a boy who sometimes returned home muddy from a school situated in a Brixton residential street. So he now misjudged sergeant Andy Devine's ability to note that Smart and Smith seemed in surprisingly good health to be attending hospital each day.

Sergeant Devine checked the MO's records noting that two days excused parade had been authorised and could have at this point merely asked to see the chit issued to the two skivers. However, suspecting that all would not be that simple - he was a naturally suspicious man - he decided to follow them, on day four of the ruse, to the out patients department and was not too surprised when it turned out to be the Cosy Cafe. Allowing time enough for them to settle he decided that a cup of tea would be just the thing.

'Morning lads'.

Erlestoke

The deception had been uncovered. Sam and Scouse were charged. Dismissed from their training course and held in detention for a month. They were then posted to Erlestoke. This was a holding camp where a squadron of Royal Engineers was being gathered prior to an overseas posting.

'Where's this overseas place then?' Scouse had asked.
'Christmas island' said the corporal in charge of the guard room.
'Where the fucks that?' Sam had asked.

CHAPTER 2

Christmas Island

Arrival

The long swoop from ten thousand feet to the unseen island runway left Sam reaching for the sick bag and wishing he'd left the orange intact. The plane landed amid a cloud of white dust that gave only glimpses of the palm trees through the windows. The orange made its presence felt but stayed down. The blinding white glare seemed to fill the plane directly the door was opened bringing with it the smell of dust and kerosene. The heat in the cabin jumped from the chilly altitude temperature to a scorching ninety degrees in moments. Sam retrieved his small pack and guitar from the rack and descended into the white glare. The runway was white, the sky seemed white but he couldn't be sure; eyes failed in the blinding sunlight. He joined the other men collecting their kitbags from the back of the plane and they shuffled off toward the marquee on the edge of the strip. In ten paces the sweat sopped at his collar, by the time he reached the tent he was drenched.

'You all right, mate?' Scouse asked, his own face dripping sweat. 'Fucking hot.' he continued, stating the obvious.

Beneath the canvas roof it seemed cooler. Permission to smoke filled the air with the scent of matches and tobacco. The tent canvas flapped and the exhausted men, their shirts dark with sweat, faces red and moist with the heat, squatted on their kitbags and smoked quietly. Sunlight blinded in from all sides. Papers on the trestle tables ruffled in the constant breeze. Christmas island shimmered all about them and not one of them could give a damn.

The army clerks checked them off against the lists. Sam went forward when his name was called then hoisted his luggage onto the baggage vehicle and waited for his friends. He lit another cigarette and surveyed the white airstrip. The plane was still parked, dazzling silver in the blinding sun. The distant palm trees looked grey in the fierce white light, all the colour seemed to have been bleached out of the scene leaving the shadows pale.

The ride into main camp was fast and bumpy and took about ten minutes. The men around him smoked and jolted as the truck sped along the white road between the dusty palms. The heat pressed through the thick canvas roof and a feeling of nausea welled up in Sam's throat. He leaned over the tail board just in case, watching the white road fly away in the dust. The arrival at the camp brought stillness and the nausea subsided.

Climbing down from the truck they retrieved their kitbags and hauled them to the tents that they were assigned. The end canvas had been rolled up and the constant breeze again brought welcome relief from the heat.

"Why' ay man, have we got to spend a whole bloody year on these things?" Geordie Thompson kicked a flimsy bed knocking it across the duckboards. He threw his kitbag on to it causing the bed to upend. 'Bloody hell!' He pushed his hand through his black curly hair, plastered to his head with sweat. 'I'll end up sleeping on the floor, man. Jeez it's hot.'

"Not strong enough to take me," Big Sid Sidley eased his bulky frame onto the canvas. "Bloody hell..." The bed creaked and the wire edges bowed ominously but it settled and held his massive weight.

Geordie peered underneath. "Never get a piss pot under there, man!" Sam laughed along with the rest but still felt too queasy to really join in. Suddenly the nausea returned. He stumbled from the tent. Having no idea where a toilet was he headed toward the grey palm trunks at the edge of the camp, scuffed through the leaf litter on the plantation floor and ended up leaning on a palm, his hand pressed against the rough grey trunk. He undid the buttons on his shirt and dragged the wet garment from his back. The sickness welled but didn't come. He leaned against the tree. The palms stretched in straight rows away from the road, the fronds, far above his head sighing in the breeze, the forest floor rustling with unseen activity. The sickness drained from his body as a large crab, one claw grown to the size of a child's hand, scraped its way across a little clear patch of sand. The stalk eyes seemed to hold Sam in their untrusting gaze. He gazed back, the boyhood fear of spiders close to his consciousness and thrust his body away from the trunk. He hurried back to the tents.

While he had been away things had changed. Bedding had been issued and sheets, a pillow and a blanket lay on his bed. He thanked Sid for the favour.

"Not at all mate. You been sick?"

"Nearly." Sam didn't feel like going into the story, land crabs or not. He lay down on the unmade canvas bed. The taste of the orange haunted for a moment then he slept, impervious to the conversation and movement all around.

Sid woke him, said it was time for tea and that he should eat something. The big man was dressed in his tropical kit. Over six foot tall and broad built Sam wondered how they had found kit to fit him.

' Makes you look a right prune,' was his judgement on the outfit. A shapeless, broad brimmed, green cotton hat perched on his head. It looked like something someone would wear as a joke. Sam donned his own outfit. Lightweight olive greens, exactly the same design that could be seen in old newsreels of the Burma campaign.

Sam put the hat on.

'How's that look?'

'Fucking stupid!' said Scouse.

They walked to the cookhouse, a large tent with a corrugated aluminium kitchen tacked onto the end. It felt comfortably familiar with the rattle of cutlery and the voices of the other men. Sam ate some mashed potato and baked beans. After the meal they lit up and talk turned to the price of cigarettes and how much it cost to get into the camp cinema.

Sam drifted outside the discussion feeling the food revive him from the last five hours. He wondered at these men; so well suited as soldiers; half way around the globe and here they were discussing the price of beer as if Charing Cross were ten minutes away.

Later, much later, he lay upon the flimsy camp bed. The orange still seemed to taste and the warm darkness was filled with the sound of those sleeping around him. The canvas still flapped like a useless sail and behind that he could hear someone sobbing, missing home or a girl. Christmas Island waited all around in the darkness.

"Tomorrow," he thought, "tomorrow..." He fell asleep.

27th March 1958

The orderly corporal woke them gently at six the next morning.

'Hands off yer cocks and on with yer socks!' Didn't matter where you were, a better wake-up call had never been devised for a bunch of twenty year olds.

Sam trailed with the rest of the men over to the line of wash basins. The morning was cool, the sky pale with the sun not yet up. He washed and shaved beneath the lights glancing left and right at the line of men bending over the zinc basins. Pink like pigs at a trough. They were moonies. Once the sun rose you had to wear your hat, had to keep in long trousers, had to use the moonies showers - the ones with the roof over - anything to keep the sun off your skin. Fifteen minutes and you were red raw.

The toilets were open plan with no doors and only the minimum of partitions between each Elsan. Made crapping difficult in the beginning but Sam had been told that you got used to it.

'End up sitting there and doing the cross word, things like "thirteen across, flowers that don't bloom in the spring, six letters," then a bit of a strain and then "blank blank vee blank blank blank," and then a sigh.'

Sam took his word for it and later managed to come up

with 'Rivers'. Flowing from springs, not blooming. Easy.

Breakfast. Like breakfast in any camp but now with the sun just rising and the cool breeze blowing through the open sides of the marquee. Clattering: eating irons on enamel plates, enamel mugs filled with sweet tea. Reconstituted powdered milk.

'Road building.' Sid finished spooning watery milk from his plate and went up for some bacon and egg.

'How d'you know all these things?' Sam asked when he got back.

'It's being tall.' Sid answered, 'corporal over there told me. Parade at half past seven and then start work. Bring your small pack, mug and eating irons.'

'How d'you build a bloody road then?' Yorkie Carr pushed his wire rimmed glasses up his reddened nose.

'Spect we'll find out.' Sid dipped bacon into his egg.

Sam ate on in silence. In his time as a Royal engineer he had built every thing and blown most of it up again. Bailey bridges by the score. These you dismantled once the exercise had finished. Things built out of wooden poles with ropes and pulleys for lifting loads. There were times when he had felt like one of those Roman slaves in the old history book pictures; always hauling and heaving and lifting. So now he would be building roads. A Roman road in the middle of the Pacific... 'The Christmas Island Way', dead straight from... where to where? The whole island was only twenty miles long and eight miles wide. Maybe they would bend it and loop it a bit. Get a few miles out of that.

They swilled their plates and threw the tea dregs into the sand as they walked back to the lines of marquees. Three or four rows of these and maybe ten to a row. Twenty men to a tent, ten each side. Wire and canvas camp beds. No furniture so most men had got hold of a small packing crate of some sort to store their kit. The side of a bigger crate could serve as a wall at your bed head that allowed some hanging space. Sam hung his guitar up and wondered how long it would be before a string went. Where do you get strings on a desert island in the middle of the

Pacific?

First parade. Much more relaxed than back home. Orders issued for the day. Remind them all that they are moonies and must avoid sunburn, a self inflicted injury in the army's book and so a chargeable offence.

Sam's squad picked out for road building and so onto the truck and set off to the work site.

Weighbatch

'Bloody hell,' Tommy Marks, a London cockney and full of it, voiced the opinion of them all as the truck turned into a site dominated by the Starmix. An enormous machine that shook and grumbled. Forty or fifty feet high, black and sooty, a vast tilted tube slowly turning amid a heat haze of tar fumes. The whole thing looked a bit like the winding gear for a coal mine with the tube replacing the angled cables. On the top, where the winding wheels would have been, there perched a rickety hut of corrugated iron complete with flagpole. A metal ladder emerged from the tangle of beams and shapes at the base and crawled up the side of the contraption to the hut. The impression was of extreme heat. If you had taken this into battle the enemy would have fled screaming. The whole thing stood in an open space with piles of crushed coral aggregate dotted about in haphazard fashion.

'You lot will be feeding that,' Corporal Chant pointed at the contraption.

'Sandwiches?' queried a voice.

'No Marks,' the corporal knew Tommy's cockney at a thousand paces, 'crushed coral, cement and tar. It loves them. Chuck them all into the top of that tube then it mixes them in the fire that shoots up the centre and produces Tarmac with which, I am sure you have guessed, Marks, we make lovely smooth roads. Smart, Sidley, Marks, Carr and Hayward; weighbatch.'

Thus Sam Smart and the others started work. Herded by a new lance corporal over to an enormous cement mixer that stood at the base of pile of crushed coral.

'The weighbatch,' the corporal indicated the biggest cement mixer any of them had ever seen, 'this makes sure that all the ingredients are accurately measured out and properly mixed.'

For the first time in Sam's life he discovered that most things were transported round the world in forty gallon oil drums; cement and tar being the diet of this site.

'Like this,' the new corporal manhandled a drum up to the big bucket then took a hand axe and chopped into the drum's metal top.

'Keep close to the edge and watch your hands on the rim, sharp as buggery once its been cut. OK, Sidley, have a go.'

Sid Sidley was six six in his socks. Could have stood in for a barn door in a storm. Not the most accurate hand with an axe, he hit the rim and sent the blade flying.

'Fer Christ's sake. You, take over,' the corporal indicated that Sam should have a go. Being five six in his socks Sam was perhaps a little nearer to the target. He started to chop, progressing the cut with each blow. The sensation was satisfying; the metal soft against the sharp axe head. It jammed.

'Side ways with the shaft,' the new corporal instructed. Sam freed the blade.

'Right, your on cutting, seem to know how to handle an axe...'

'Always handy with his chopper...' Tommy Marks never missed a joke. The other lads laughed and the new corporal smiled and continued his demonstration.

The lesson was over quickly and the work routine began. The sun climbed higher in the sky and the sweat began to darken the olive green jackets and trousers. The team took it in turns to chop and haul and empty the cement into the mixer. The coral was added until the weight was right then the whole was dry mixed and emptied into dumpers then driven off toward the starmix.

Infantry men carry their rifles with them wherever they

go or so the army would like you to believe. Sappers carry a jack knife. Black handle, single blade and a marlin spike. This spike is used to splice ropes. Or so the army would have you believe. Sam had observed that in reality the spike was used to punch holes in tins of evaporated milk. Had also observed that the whole knife become the focus of every inspection. Any sergeant wanting to deal out a bit of discipline would home in on the jack knife that repository of grime held bumping on the left buttock by a white lanyard that looped around the waist. You didn't use your jack knife, you kept it clean. The other item that sappers carried about was an enamel mug. In the days before plentiful plastic cups the enamel mug was the only means of getting tea into yourself. The milk was always evaporated, always poured from a twice spiked tin.

Tea break was at ten in the morning and the five men trouped off with the new corporal for a rest.

Work sites are always made comfortable by the people who work in them. This one had a tent roof and boxes for chairs. Out of the sun they sat, sipped tea and smoked.

Sam thought of taking his jacket off but the thought of putting the sweat sodden thing back on stopped him.

'How long do we have to keep wearing these, corp?'

'Till you get acclimatised. Take it steady. Late sun is best that way you know the light is always going down. Had a guy a month ago skived of site for a smoke and fell asleep. Blisters the size of your small pack poor sod. No. Leave it till late and then not too long.'

The sound of a plane approached and the corporal covered his tea and told them to do the same. The plane, an Auster, roared low overhead.

'Mr Flit,' he explained. Wait for it,' A light mist of insect killer drifted down with the unmistakable smell of Flit.

'Kills the mozzies and ruins your tea if you don't keep it out.'

'You got a name, corp?' Sid put the question.

'Kitchener, and your country could do with you lot back to work; shift!'

CHAPTER 3

Life in Camp

Lunch

For the first couple of weeks Sam and the squad worked up to one o'clock then got into the truck for the swimming lagoon, this cleaned the cement dust from their skin. Then the truck took them to the cookhouse for dinner.

'Lunch is for officers and other toffs,' Sam had been told, 'other ranks have dinner mid day.'

These hours were loosely referred to as 'Ghurkha hours'. Salt tablets became part of the diet. Hot meals were always served with much talk of them being cooling.

'That's why the Indians eat curry and not salad,' Scouse was full of useless information. 'The curry makes you sweat and that cools you down. Bloody obvious really.' He sat back and grinned, his chubby face a caricature of happiness. You never knew if he was joking or not. His crew cut hair spiked upwards as if he was constantly connected to the electricity main.

'And they drink tea in glasses,' Yorkie Carr added.

'They all got bad eyes then?' Tommy Marks had a cranked view of the world.

The conversation followed it's usual meandering path, constantly directed into a new direction by wisecracks. The squadron had been together as a whole for about three of four months now and they all knew each other in a way that only comes from shared hardship: army life was considered generally bad, to be born rather than enjoyed. They came from all over the country bringing with them the customs and idioms from home. Sam, a Londoner as was Tommy Marks. Scouse from Huyton near Liverpool. Yorkie Carr from somewhere in Yorkshire. Robbie Robinson from Malta! and big Sid Sidley from Didcot...

'In Wiltshire, big railway sidings,' he had explained and Sam had wondered if he should be impressed. Before joining the army the only place that Sam had known outside London was

Liverpool and that only because his Dad had been posted to a fort in the Mersey. Where the place was he had not the faintest idea. Scouse Smith and another Scouser, Downey, had impressed him with their humour and their clipped Liverpudlean accent.

Jim Haywood was a mystery man, he seemed to have lived everywhere but had claimed none of the places as home.

'Southerner,' Yorkie had pronounced which had seemed to position it precisely enough for a Yorkshireman.

All these men had been gathered at Erlestoke and mixed in with the other characters. Keeny, Tinsley and others. Some Sam had met before, others were new. He had left friends behind at every stage. Loft Beattie had moved on from training camp to lord knows where. He had been a good mate along with Robbie and before Scouse. The constant posting from place to place led to a complete serendipity of friends who one stumbled across from time to time during ones service.

Sam tucked in to his Irish stew, English food. On the journey out they had experienced American food. Very different.

The Journey out

It had taken about two days to get here, maybe more. Date lines and time differences had blurred the days. A short flight to Shannon in Ireland then the long Atlantic crossing seated above the wing with Geordie Thompson thinking the engines were on fire all the time.

New York and Sam's first experience of automatic doors. The Americans took them for granted, wouldn't push when a faulty one didn't open. Just walked at it again then chose another one. Amazing in Sam's view. The airport, Idlewild, was grey and the weather wet.

They were given a food voucher and Sam made his way to the restaurant and ordered something that he thought may be light: a steak sandwich. When it arrived he was astounded. Two halves of big bread bun filled the centre of an oval plate with a steak draped across them. At each end of the plate a salad and in little dimples around the plate's rim pickles and sauces. The whole thing about the size of a Sunday roast back home. No, bigger! He struggled through, manfully.

Next a Pan Am to San Francisco. American airhostesses. Glamorous, kind and knowing.

'You guys need cheering up,' she was tall and blonde with big eyes and a little blue hat, 'I have just the thing...' The 'guys' all raised their eyebrows...

'Here,' she wheeled in a huge box trolley and dished out American comics. They were brilliant.

The flight across America had been long. Sam had stared out of the window following the track of a straight road. He had kept his eye on this road for about four hours. It never deviated and he never saw a single vehicle on it. Eventually he fell asleep to awake after the sun had set and the plane was landing in San Francisco. Weary and disorientated they wandered over to the terminal.

The luxury of San Francisco airport had only ever been seen in films. A car was displayed on a brightly lit stage, tilted at an angle to enable the interior to be seen. The car was straight out of the movies, long and black and with fins. The whole place resembled a film set. Sam had wandered out onto a balcony with a root beer - how American was that! - and smelled orange blossom for the first time in his life. A moment and a fragrance that would stay with him forever.

From San Francisco down to Hawaii and the beginning of air sickness. From Hawaii to Christmas island with feelings of nausea and the taste of orange.

Cookhouse

Back in the cookhouse Robbie Robinson wandered over with his lunch and joined them.

'Where've you been?' Sam asked.

'Wiring to be done. You should have been a sparks, mate. No humping loads for me, just a nice little wiring job in the officers mess.'

'Jammy bugger,' Sam and Robbie were best mates. Sam envied Robbie's style. The guy had black hair and brown eyes; always dressed smart, blazer and flannels. He had been born in Malta and Sam suspected that he was half Maltese but he had never asked. Already he looked tanned while the others were red.

'And you still get to knock off at lunch time?'
'Too right, mate, I'm exhausted.'

The big cookhouse tent reminded Sam of a circus tent. The thick poles supporting the roof were painted red, the tent itself was white. At half past one you could feel the sun's heat pushing through the canvas. The side panels had been rolled up in places and the whole structure flapped in the constant breeze.

'Trade winds, they blow most of the year,' Lionel Rose, the brains of the squad had explained. 'Called trade winds because they enabled sailing ships to navigate the globe and trade.'

'You're a clever bugger Lionel,' said Tommy Marks. Sam reflected that he had known about the trade winds but that it was better that Lionel told the others.

The days began to drag. Sam ticked his 'days to do' chart. The long awaited tan finally arrived enabling them to strip to the waist, wear shorts and shower in the open showers. They discovered the different kinds of water. Salt from the sea, Raw that had been filtered, Banana from the ground - wells in the middle of the island - and drinking water. Raw water was good enough for showering. 'Sea water soap' became the thing; it would lather in sea water.

Sam gradually settled himself in getting a decent crate side to make his 'wall' at the head of his bed. He pinned his 'days to do' chart onto this and began ticking off the three hundred and sixty odd days that he reckoned would comprise his tour. Maybe it was the distinct absence of women but he noticed that there were very few pin ups. Starving men don't hoard pictures of pies.

Lionel was right; the wind never stopped. The flap, flap, flap of canvas became the background sound. The white of the sand and the sky became the daylight and the blaze of the milky way lit the night with an eerie glow. The breakers beat against the reef a hundred yards from the beach, a deep sigh that took over from the flapping canvas once you left the tents.

Some men still sobbed in the darkness but Sam was self sufficient; no girl friends left behind just a step mother that didn't see eye to eye with him. He smoked and played his guitar learning the three big chords that Louis Patchittie had taught him. E, A and B7.

The Naafi.

Sam wasn't a drinker. Beer was nice rather than necessary so the NAAFI came as a surprise. The Naafi was huge; really a hangar with metal funiture and a long bar with an even longer queue for beer. No spirits.

'They never serve OR's spirits,' Sid led the way to the bar, 'other ranks could get out of hand and so it's just beer for us, keeps our intake per hour lower'.

'I could just go a whisky,' said Robbie.

The queue was really long. Sam looked about him. The metal tables and chairs provided little comfort, not that comfort was an issue; these men were young and tired from the work and heat of the day. Cold beer straight from the can overrode any idea of comfort. Men smoking, talking, drinking beer. No women and therefore no friction: plenty of beer, plenty of cigarettes. No fighting. Sam liked the idea of this big homogenous group of happy men; nothing to prove; relaxed.

'Best get a box,' Scouse indicated the front of the queue, 'by the time we're finished a couple of cans you'd have to be at the back of the queue again. How many cans in a box, skin?' he asked a brawny lad with two boxes.

'Twenty four, mate.'

'Six each, yeah,'

Sam wondered if he could manage six cans. Scouse saw the hesitation.

'Don't worry Sam, if you can't manage I'll help you out!'

'OK' get a box Sid,' said Sam, 'we'll get a table. Pay you back later.'

The back end of the Naafi hangar served food, hot dogs, burgers, chips. Robbie and Scouse did a recce.

'American style hamburgers,' Scouse needed feeding. He

was a chubby guy. Probably the nicest man one would ever meet despite the tough looking exterior: short cropped blond hair topped his heavy frame. He had more jokes than any of them.

Sam slipped Robbie the money and watched as they snaked through the tables picking up Sid's order on the way.

A crash over at the far corner drew his attention. A great pile of empty cans had been knocked over; probably by a rival tower builder Sam later learned. The empties were carefully stacked to create great Pisa like towers; the lean became their downfall. 'The straight towers of Piss-up', a nice idea, Sam thought. The concrete floor of the Naafi was one of the few places that this could be done. Everywhere else was sand and duckboards. Most of the day was spent walking on sand, soft, fine white coral sand. The stuff of books about desert islands. None of the books mentioned it's less appealing properties. If it got into a wound it gave you coral poisoning. Not life threatening - you had to see the medic straight away so it didn't have a chance - but it would look bad and itch like mad making sleeping a nightmare. The point was that when on duty you had to wear boots and puttees; these to stop the sand getting into the boots. Looked ridiculous at first but like most things, you got used to it.

The other thing was sunburn. You had to wear your hat and keep covered up for the first few weeks but there was no way of sheltering the eye lids and beneath your eyebrows from the reflected glare and they had all suffered the burning sensation that came with every blink of the eye. The cheap suntan lotion on offer in the Naafi shop went some way to alleviating the pain but it was relentless and caught you off guard at times.

Sid was coming back with the box of beer, Scouse and Robbie were nearly being served. Maybe it wasn't so bad to be on a desert island with such friends even if it was not like in the books.

The 'burgers were great made even greater with Del Monte Tomato ketchup. Sam began to realise how austere Britain still was in the late fifties. Maybe it was being in the army that made it seem as if nothing were changing. In fifty three, when Sam had joined as a boy soldier, a lot of the senior ranks had come from those left over from the war. These men were too old for the modern fighting army and had been charged with the task of looking after boy soldiers. Sam remembered Bob, the trumpet major. Bald as a coot this man was old and kind and still dressed in the uniform of the first world war; peaked cap and a tunic rather than a battledress blouse. He wore puttees but they were wound up his legs as the men in the trenches had worn them. And 'Trumpet Major'? what sort of a rank was that? Maybe it was this hanging on to the past that made progress seem totally absent. And now...

Well now he was sitting in a corrugated aluminium hanger eating American hamburgers with American ketchup and listening to rock and roll from the speakers. Not only that but they were all gathered to witness the testing of H bombs and A bombs. They had spent two days in modern airplanes getting here, had spanned the 'states and even landed in Hawaii. The stuff of fantasy.

'Tennents lager mate, gerit down yer. Right,' Scouse launched into a joke. 'There,s this lad walkin' down Lime street and a prossy stops him "want sumtin nice" she asks and the lad says ok and goes with her and catches a dose of clap. Six months later he's cured and walking down Lime street again and the same prossy stops him; "want sumtin new?" she asks. "What the fuck you got now?" he says, " leprosy!" '

They all laugh and another joke begins. Sam's thoughts drift back to the events that brought him to the middle of the Pacific ocean. Him and Scouse; partners in crime.

The alteration of nine to nineteen plan to avoid first parade at Brompton barracks had, thinking back, been a mistake.

It was a crap plan but neither of them could see that and so they had avoided the dreaded Brompton Barracks first parade and sloped off to the 'Cosy Cafe' in Brompton High Street to take a leisurely tea and toast, a welcome addition to their cookhouse breakfast. Early elevenses.

The 'Cosy' was well worth the effort. Nev, the owner, a tall thin man with a sculpted nose and chin, far too noble for a mere cafe owner, had proved a generous soul employing Sam two evenings a week to help out with cleaning the tables and washing up. The juke box pumped out music all evening - Paul Anka singing 'Diana' forty nine times one night - and everybody who was anybody dropped in at one time or another. Money was always the problem. The pawn shop across the way did a brisk trade in tools - Brompton was a trades training barracks and so tool boxes could be hocked to improve the financial position at the beginning of the week. Harry Street would come in and peruse the racing pages placing imaginary bets which he wrote in the margin. In theory he was good and won large but imaginary amounts. He would sit there and click two half crowns together and offer the loan of a pound for the repayment of a pound and a shilling.

'A guinea, you twonks!' he would correct men as they worked out his interest rate.

Well the crap plan had failed; Sam and Scouse had been hauled up in front of the CO and charged with being absent from parade. It was all quite hazy as he thought about it now.

It had been a chaotic business with 'The Beast' - Brompton's provost sergeant, - getting witnesses muddled up. Sam had been marched into the big room, central to the Victorian facade, that served as the CO's court room. Filing in they had crossed the back of the room and halted then turned right and advanced as a rank toward the enormous desk. Sam in the middle flanked by two guards and witnesses. Silence had followed the final halt and the charge had been read out. The problem was that Sam knew he was with Scouse's witness's. As the charge was read out Sam realised the CO had Scouse's charge sheet in front of him.

The procedure was halted and the room cleared. More chaos followed.

It has to be understood that as a prisoner no word could be spoken until it was called for. The same applied to witnesses. Those that knew remained mute and as none of the participants were known by sight to the provost sergeant and his guards the pantomime continued with a timing and grace that would have made a farce writer weep with joy.

Scouse had skidded on the polished floor and slid beneath the knee hole desk at one point. Sam had declared the court a shambles at another and earned himself a week's solitary confinement before serving the other three weeks in the cells of Kitchener barracks.

The solitary had been an experience. Cold had ensured that he could now do a hundred and twenty press ups with ease. A corporal had smuggled in the middle two hundred odd pages of a paperback, and so the physical exercise kept him warm and the mental exercise of working out the beginning and end of the story kept him sane. It would probably have sparked a literary career in Sam but without a pencil it remained only a mental exercise.

Finally they had been shipped off to Devises to await postings. Well Erlestoke in reality. The middle of nowhere would have been an accurate location, not near anywhere was the general description of the camp. A vast square edged with wooden huts marked it's centre and February was a particularly cold month that year. Any prisoner of war film would have furnished the reader with it's description. It existed, like a film, in black and white with greys which a film director would have loved. The population of the camp grew daily with fresh arrivals from the vast unseen Corps of Royal Engineers. Very little happened but new friends were made. Sam and Scouse went out on the Friday evening to Trowbridge and a 'hop' in the town hall.

'Drink up, mate,' Scouse handed Sam the opener and the noise of the vast Naafi hanger came back up. The piles of cans were getting higher and the cold lager was beginning to have an effect. 'Pictures tomorrow, costs a shilling to get in.' Everybody knew more than Sam. It seemed to him that they knew the plot right from the beginning. He just stumbled along and improvised. So they would go to the pictures tomorrow evening.

The Cinema

Like everything else on the island the cinema was made of corrugated aluminium with duck boards and seats. Run by the Army Kinema Corporation it was a shilling in the front half of the auditorium and one and six in the slightly raised back half. There was no roof. The show followed the pattern of all cinemas. Occasional newsreels, three cartoons and then the big picture. There never was a B movie second feature as it was considered that the three cartoons were B feature enough for the sometimes rowdy male audience.

Because of the absence of the roof the start of the performance was dictated by the setting of the sun and so as the sky darkened the show would begin. The high arch of the heavens would put to shame the ceilings of any Gaumont or Odion back home. Sam, Sid, Scouse and Robbie decided on the one and six's and made themselves comfortable with their two cans - it was the rule, only two cans per performance - tucked between their feet. Short sighted Geordie and Yorkie Carr paid a shilling and sat just below the screen.

'Carve 'er name with Pride, this'll be good,' Scouse had optimism built in.

'Wonder where he'll carver 'er name?'

'On a palm tree, most like', Sid noted.

'No palm trees in France,' Robbie chipped in.

'Ow'd you know it's in France,' asked Sid.

'Seen it. Went up London, saw it when it first came out.'

'Is it good?' asked Scouse. Robbie grinned.

A newsreel about an anti nuclear weapons march started the show and received cheers but it didn't seem likely that they would achieve much to affect Sam's posting.

Everything was a bit out of date really.

'International date line,' Lionel explained later, 'we're in Monday while back home it's still Sunday.'

'So,' said Jackie Bones his broad Newcastle accent taking on a pensive tone, 'when it's Sunday here it's Saturday back home?'

Jackie Bones was thin and claimed to have one leg shorter than the other. How they had failed to notice when he joined up he never knew. With Chic Brown, a Glaswegian, they made a team that knew all there was to be known about league football. They would answer correctly the most obscure teasers, would reel off cupfinal scores from the turn of the century often boasting that the Royal Engineers had won the trophy in eighteen seventy five!

'Yes,' Lionel hoped that any reasoning to come would be a bit quicker.

'So Saturday here...' Jackie paused and they all leaned forward, 'is Friday at home and on Saturday afternoon when the lads kick off I'm in Sunday and I know the result while they are still playin' and if I could get me coupon in...' The assembled brains began to wrestle with the problem.

'Yeah but,' Tommy Marks chipped in, 'even if you knew the result your coupon would take a couple of days to get home. Too late, you're knackered.'

'I could phone me mam,' Jackie was determined that the scheme would work.

'How would you find the results out in the first place, then?' Sid had leaned into the conversation.

'On the radio.'

'Being broadcast yesterday...' Tommy was still interested 'Aye.'

'So they get to the end of they match and say 'Sunderland three, Queens Park Rangers three and you ring your Mam and tell her to put it down as a score draw and she rushes round to Littlewoods and puts the coupon on the desk and...'

'Waits for the end of the game...' Sid looked puzzled.

'Nah, QPR'd never draw with Sunderland.' Tommy was on firmer ground now. 'thrash them, beat 'em hollow.'

Sam listened as the conversation drifted into football mode. He had never understood the fascination that it held for people. The only time he had ever had anything to do with the game was when, as a six year old, he had been walking beside a pitch and a ball had come over and hit him on the head, spattering mud on his face. The players who ran over, slightly older than him, had scowled as if he should have done something with it like scored a goal maybe. He had avoided the game ever since.

After the newsreel came the cartoons. Three in a row and at the end of each one a 'That's all Folks'. Then 'Fred Quimby' - the producer - came up on the screen and the audience bellowed the name as one. Four and a half thousand men on a desert island with wives and girlfriends thousands of miles away. 'Quimby' was as close as they would get to the female form for a long time.

Music matters

Peggy Sue was coming along nicely. Sam sat on his bedside box and wrestled his way through the chords. E then A then E by way of introduction. In his head Buddy Holly's voice would hiccup it's way in here. Sam sang for him.
'Peggy Sue, Peggy Sue, da da da da da de doo, Oh Peggy, my Peggy Su u ooo '. The dum diddly dum from the record thrummed in his head and Terry Ogilvy in the next bed said 'You ought to learn the words really, you're just singing the title,' which Sam felt was unhelpful as he had neither sheet music nor record.
'Mmm,' he replied and twisted his fingers to get the B7 chord.
The guitar was a Voss. Seven pounds from a second hand shop in Balham high road. Louis Patchittie had helped with the first steps: tuning and e major comprising the first lesson. From then on the aim had been to change from one chord to the next without looking. Easier said than done but at least now his fingers had hardened, stopped stinging.
'Do you reckon you'll ever learn to play that thing?' Terry continued.
'Well, it can't be that difficult. Loads of rock 'n rollers thrumming away'.
'You should get the Bert Weedon book, my mate did and he's in a skiffle group back home in Southampton. Does all the

Lonny Donigan stuff in a club just down by the Bargate.'

Terry often went on about the Bargate. Sam had a picture in his mind of a barrier across a road but couldn't imagine a barrier as being something worth crowing about; moaning about yes.

'What's the Bargate?' he asked.

'It's an old gate, big mind you, like a castle with battlements on top. Goes across the high street. Trams used to go through it but that stopped and the busses have to go round it now. Great place. There's a coffee bar called the Check Point down in a cellar right next to it'.

'Do they do skiffle in the Check Point then?'

'No, too posh for that. Well not posh, intimate. I take my bird Doreen down there; subdued lighting and all that. Gets her in the mood.'

Not having any one to get in the mood, Sam tried a B7 chord again.

CHAPTER 4

Work

Tar Kettles

The gang; Sam Smart, Sid Sidley, Tommy Marks, Yorkie Carr and Jim Hayward, now got rotated to work on the Tar Kettles. Two kettles each.

'Here we go again,' thought Sam as Corporal Kitchener handed them over to their new boss who immediately launched into the method of opening a forty gallon drum of tar. This time you cut a trap door in the side, where the air pocket was, the barrels having been stored on their side. Sam got the hang of that fairly quickly tapping the back of the axe on the metal to find the pocket.

The kettles looked just like Stephenson's Rocket but

without the piston assembly. Four iron wheels, a tall smoke stack at one end and a fire box opening at the other. Looked at from the end the contraption was a U shaped affair. Two barrels would be hoisted aboard. Undo the hoist hooks and roll the first on along the guides about half way. Legs apart looking down into the pool of molten tar as you hacked an opening in the side then rolled the barrel one more turn to let the tar drain out. The black pool of tar bubbled and spat as Sam's sweat dripped into it.

'Don't fall in, mate,' shouted Sid on his way past, 'get covered and we'll have to call you Sambo!'

Sam made sure his boots pushed firmly against the sides of the kettle.

The kettles were a bit easier than the weigh batch. All the heavy work was done by the mobile crane which hoisted the barrels onto the kettle. Once the reservoir was full the tanker pumped the hot tar out and took it across to the Starmix. As the day wore on the lads would keep an eye on the Starmix flagpole which topped off the corrugated aluminium hut on top of the monster. With luck, before tea break a pair of stockings would be hauled up. First ton of the shift. The black nylons would fly well in the breeze that had propelled Captain Cook around the world. The second ton would be the suspender belt. Again black. A pair of knickers would follow and, myth had it that the squadron before had managed to hoist the brassier, an ample garment again in black.

Sam wondered how the underwear had found it's way onto the island. It certainly didn't look to be the sort of stuff either of the two WVS women would wear.

'One's sixty and the other one has a limp.' was the standard description. Tommy Marks had wondered how old the other one was and, more importantly, how she had got the limp. That was the thing with Tommy, always in with a chance even against four thousand four hundred and ninety nine men.

'Well ninety eight really,' Lionel calculated that the CO would be happy with the sixty year old.

Tea break rolled round. The nylons fluttered and Sam could swear he heard Mr Flit taking off. The big urn stood waiting like an oasis. He poured himself a mug and sat down opening a fresh tin of State Express ciggies. The round tins were a miracle really. You pulled a little metal tag to the edge of the tin then gave the lid a twist which opened the silver foil and revealed fifty tightly packed cigarettes. At two and six for fifty you could smoke yourself silly. He lit up and took a swig of tea.

'Shit!' It was salty. 'Who made the tea?'

'Me. What's wrong with it?' Yorkie Carr pushed his glasses up his nose and sipped from his own mug pulling a face.

'Oh bugger, I've made it with raw water. I'll have...' the rest of the sentence was drowned out with the roar of the Auster as Mr Flit dusted them down with DDT. Sam put his hand over the mug of salty tea. Reflex action really.

They all cursed Yorkie who set off to make a fresh brew while they went back to work. Half an hour later they sat down to a proper mug of tea and without the attentions of Mr Flit.

'I wonder why we don't take a break this time every day,' mused Lionel.

'Tradition' said Sid.

Barber Greene

The Barber Greene machine laid the tarmac. They'd watched it working one day while they were off shift.

The sergeant in charge of the machine, glad to be asked, had explained the theory behind road making. The scrapers flattening the base, then the crushed coral bed pummelled flat by sheep's foot rollers: little feet sticking out rather than just a smooth roller.

'Like air hostesses aren't allowed to wear stilettos,' he explained, 'the tiny footprint would deliver about a ton of weigh to an aircraft floor. Concentrated. Same with the roller. Lots of little feet.'

Once the white ribbon of coral was sufficiently compacted along would come the Barber Greene. Half the road width it would follow the tarmac truck and lay a broad, flat blanket of Macadam that steamed even in the island's equatorial heat. The smooth road roller would follow making the black ribbon gleam.

'Romans were buggered without tarmac,' the sergeant explained proudly, 'had to put in long stones on end to bed the road in. Still didn't work. Rain seeps in, freezes and you're buggered. Pot hole in no time. The secret is that tarmac is water proof. Keeps the base dry.'

Sid said later that he had been tempted to mention that freezing rain was scarce as rocking horse shit out here but had decided to keep quiet about it.

Back in camp

Quiet and letter

Sam got an airmail blank and settled down to compose a rare letter to his step mother, Grace, back in Tooting. What to write? He felt like a school boy being asked what he had learned at school today. 'Nothing.' The classic reply and yet here he was on a desert island. White sand, palm trees. No Hula Hula girls true but... nothing.

Grace didn't seem to be on his thinking level at all. She was very proper. When he was younger he had always wanted to visit her sister's house on a Sunday afternoon but Grace had always insisted that they be invited. As a thirteen year old Sam had struggled with the problem of letting auntie Elsie know that he wanted to be invited so that she could let Grace know. The trouble with that was that while Elsie had a phone, Grace did not. He realised the shortcomings in the plan. It would look suspicious him coming from the phone booth in Franciscan road to pass the message on. Once he had joined the army things got a bit worse. As a fifteen year old boy soldier he felt independent.

'Not while you're in this house young man.' And so the pair of them had niggled away at each other. Dad had acted as oil between them but Sam realised he was a disappointment to her and had no idea how to change that.

'Dear Mum,' he wrote.

The canvas flapped and Jim Hayward sat picking gently

on Sam's guitar, his fingers red raw with the constant pressure.

Suddenly shouting. Sam rushed outside and at first couldn't make out what was happening. Jim and Sid joined him. No one was to be seen but it then dawned on them that the next marquee was not there or rather it was there and heaving like a stricken animal as the occupants frantically tried to crawl out from beneath it. Only the three main tent poles stood naked against the sky. The canvas had rotted sufficiently to lose its grip on the ropes. They waded in and began to peel the canvas away from the struggling men.

'Anyone hurt in there?' yelled Sid as he hauled at the canvas revealing first one then more of the men. Beds were upended, kit strewn about.

'I'll get the orderly officer,' said Lionel and shot off toward the guardroom.

'All the canvas has rotted at the top of the polls. Everything fucking rots on this fucking island.' Jim hauled at the heavy brown canvas, untangling the mess of guy ropes and wooden pegs.

'It was true,' thought Sam, a good proportion of those swimming did so naked'. It was when his own trunks came apart at the seam that he realised why.

'Sea water,' he had guessed.

'Sun more likely,' said Lionel. 'Sun, coral and wind. Sun gets rid of the oils in the material, fine coral dust gets in and the wind moves the ever more brittle fibres causing them to break.'

'Evah more brittle... whooo Lionel,' said Tommy Marks.

The afternoon became chaotic as a new marquee was fetched from the stores and they were all commandeered to clear the old one and erect the new.

Sam went back to his airmail form.

'The tent next to ours collapsed today,' he wrote.

The tests.

'I reckon it'll be a Vulcan. Bloody brilliant 'plane that,' Yorkie Carr cleaned his glasses, 'better than the Victor and the Valiant put together. I mean what sort of a name is Victor for a bomber? Victor Sylvester?

'Victor Hugo,' added Lionel. 'French...'

'He plays for Sunderland don't he? Tommy Marks lowered the tone.

'He bloody does not!' Mickey Doyle, joined in. Mickey was from Sunderland and so Sam felt that he should know.

'Why does everything come back to football? Sam asked.

'Because it's the best thing next to women and we haven't got any women so football it is.

Tommy's explanation had that Tommy logic to it. Sam wondered what his background was. A Londoner who sprinkled his conversation with Cockney rhyming slang. Once noting that his mate had a 'jam jar' he had left them all puzzled until he explained that it was a 'car'.

'Little car, jam jar; get a bigger one and it's a la de dah. My dad speaks it all the time, silly bugger.'

The conversation followed it's steady meander and Sam began to wonder about the tests. The fact that they had come out here to build roads and huts had been accepted as a fact in itself. Why these things were being built never seemed to be questioned; almost as if someone had decided it would be a good idea to pave a desert island over just for the hell of it. Nobody had really mentioned the tests and yet that was the whole point of the place. Later they would become known as Nuclear tests; right now they were atom bomb tests, nice late fifties speak. Atom bombs. The first one for these was scheduled for next Monday, twenty eighth of April.

'Buy a Thermos flask,' Sid had advised,' I've been told these things go on for hours and they don't have a tea break. Stops you pissing,' he added, "don't drink, don't pee'.

Monday morning saw the tea urns being emptied at a rate of knots as Thermos's were filled. After first parade Sam marched with the others to a vast open space and sat down on the sand grass in the squadron's allotted space.

'Nice day for it,' Robbie lit up and blew a plume of smoke into the cool morning air lifting his chin and closing his eyes.

'First fag of the day should always be taken after one has finished ones' ablutions and breakfasted. Allow all that to pass and the body is ready for the calming nicotine,' he had explained. Sam's envy had increased. His routine was to get up, light up then cough. Only after all these things did ablutions and breakfast get a look in.

Jazz blared over the loud speakers. Sam didn't mind jazz as long as it was trad. The modern stuff seemed to be a bit either chaotic or pretentious. All off tune sax's or vibraphones in the mist was his opinion. Chris Barber now; there was something and Lonny Donegan. Great.

'Fire house five plus two.' Once more Lionel knew. 'They draw cartoons for Walt Disney.

'Plus two?,' queried Sam.

'Used to be five then two more came along,' explained Lionel as if that were answer enough. 'They play the jazz so that we know the Tannoy system is still working. If it goes silent within the drop period we have to face away and cover our eyes. We won't know when it's happening without the count down.'

'Good job you're here, Lionel,' said Tommy, 'we'd all be fucked otherwise!'

The jazz played on for about an hour. Sid slid off to chat to a mate from another squadron.

'Make sure you unscrew the top of your Thermos when the bombs been dropped. The blast buggers the inside otherwise. Pete Cunningham told me.'

'He's seen it all before?'

'Yeah, reckons it pretty impressive once you get to see it.'

The jazz stopped.

'The aircraft are on the approach run.' came over the Tannoy. The jazz resumed.

'What would happen if they dropped the bomb in the wrong place, say here?' Jim Haywood wondered.

'You could skive off getting a haircut,' Sam told him, 'and you'd never finish learning the guitar; all that fingertip hardening for nothing.'

'Same applies,' said Jim.

'With the subtle difference that I don't need a haircut,' said Sam, pushing his hand through his short crew cut.

The sun was gaining height and the temperature

climbing when the Tannoy promised the aircraft would soon be in sight flying up from the south. All eyes began to search the horizon as the Fire House Five launched into Tiger Rag for the fifteenth time.

A cheer went up as a distant vapour trail climbed the blue dome of the sky. Two more appeared and the three made agonisingly slow progress towards the gathered men. The jazz stopped as the trails grew higher. 'The weapon has left the 'plane. Two minutes and counting'.

'Bloody hell,' said Jim, 'told you they'd drop it in the wrong place! That means that somewhere between that 'plane which has still some way to go before it is over head and us there's a bloody big hydrogen bomb!'

'One minute thirty seconds and counting,' Tiger Rag resumed and Sam imagined the bomb on it's downward trajectory. All the little timing devices - a memory of some film or other - spinning toward zero as the weapon headed for its own destruction

'One minute...turn away from target area.'

'fifty seconds...'

'Cover your eyes,' the shout went up from the officers and sergeants. Sam hunched crossed legged then remembered the flask lid. He unscrewed it with his eyes closed, a sense of urgent fear suddenly gripped, ignoring the countdown.

'Twenty... Ten... five, four three two one, zero, one, two...' The count up began, and a warm glow travelled up Sam's back, as if someone had switched on an electric fire behind him. He could see the light through his fingers and remembered shining a torch through his hand as a child, seeing the rosy light in the darkness of his bedroom. This was brighter and then it faded. Not really a flash more a raising of the lights and then back down again.

'You may turn and face the target area.'

Sam shuffled round, still sitting. An enormous sun rose above the palm trees, golden, hard to look at. Suddenly it milked over; egg yolk turning white in hot water...

'Stand by for blast.'

The palm trees whipped as if the island had hit a rock

and a loud crack left them all slightly deafened. Silence followed as they all gaped at the mushroom cloud that was beginning to climb higher by the second. It was massive.

'Fag?' Robbie held a cigarette out for Sam then proffered a light.

Sam inhaled and knew that he had seen something he would never forget.

The Tannoy fell silent, it seemed the island fell silent; only a faint rumble could be heard, a distant thunder from within the cloud.

CHAPTER 5

After the first bomb

Swimming

'The rest of the day is ours,' Sid poured tea from his flask, 'I wonder how many got smashed?'

'His did.' A disgruntled squaddy rattled a Thermos, the broken glass sloshing about inside. Gradually they got up and began the wandering that crowds do when the show is over. Sam headed back toward main camp sipping his tea as he went. The rumbling cloud still climbed but slowly now, beginning to deform.

'We've joined a special club now,' Lionel fell in beside him, 'not many people in the world have witnessed what we've just seen.'

'I suppose not. The poor buggers in Japan didn't live to tell the tale, did they?'

'The ones that did are the unlucky ones,' said Lionel.

Sam could see the truth in that. Radiation was bad because you couldn't see it. Ordinary bombs went off; buildings collapsed then that was it. Invisible radiation, that was different. His mind groped toward an idea. Deterrent. That was the big word. Automatic weapons systems: you bomb me and my bombs are on their way. What was the answer to that? Invisible radiation everywhere. Who'd won?

'Fancy a swim?' Scouse caught them up.

'Yep. Drop this and get my flippers.' The big ideas faded into thoughts of swimming.

The swimming lagoon was a vast circle of water open at one end to further lagoons where, it was rumoured, the big sharks lurked. The entrance from those lagoons was protected by a shark net: a steel wire net that, it was rumoured again, had rusted to uselessness just below the water's surface.

In the middle of the swimming lagoon was a raft, twelve by twelve feet, moored and carpeted with coconut matting. A low diving board lifted the diver three feet or so above the water.

One side of the lagoon boasted a white sandy beach but the opposite side was bounded, to the water's edge, by palm trees and was muddy. Sam had swum over there once but, when he gained the shade of the trees with the soft white mud beneath his feet he had become anxious. It was very quiet with no breeze. It seemed sinister.

During their time on the weigh batch they had enjoyed an afternoon swim courtesy of the MO. The medics had discovered that only salt water would break down the cement dust that got into the pores and so after each shift they had got into the truck and been driven to the swimming lagoon where they had swum in the salty water. As with all daily things the trip had soon acquired its own ritual. Strip off in the truck then race down the short beach, naked as Adam before the fall. Whoops and shouts as the strong swimmers, led by Big Sid, struck out for the raft. About half way between beach and raft the cry would go up 'Nobby Clarke!' - Tommy speak for Shark - this would add an urgency to the swim. Sam remembered running with his mates in the dark, back in his school days. All frightened of some unknown thing chasing them. The fact that he was naked and that anything wishing to eat him had to start somewhere... He swam the harder.

Sid, invariably first, would haul himself up onto the raft,

leap onto the diving board then launch himself in for the return journey.

The ritual had descended into chaos one day. All eyes being wide open for any sign of a shark had missed an addition to the scene. Three beautiful women basked on the diving raft. Bikinied as only American air hostesses could be. Sun glasses bigger than Sam had ever seen; maybe a secondary observation. Sid hauled up then froze. Other swimmers now sought to take advantage of Sid's apparent loss of interest in the race. They hauled themselves up bundling the big man forward. The front runners then froze. The air hostesses froze. Sam wondered later whether any of them had been dreaming about something exotic and romantic happening on a palm fringed lagoon. The stumbling embarrassment that now played out on the twelve by twelve stage would hardly be a fitting end to such a dream.

A communal diving in now took place. Men and hostesses sought the privacy of the water. 'Adam after the fall,' thought Sam later..."*and they knew they were naked...*"

The confusion continued even when the beach was reached. The back of the truck lay twenty yards off.

Not being a particularly powerful swimmer, Sam had observed the confusion from the safety of the water. Sharks were forgotten as his gaze took in the well filled bikini tops. How long since he had seen a woman?

From this had arisen the 'Air Hostess Forecast.' Camp radio would announce the arrival of females which would give rise to many imagined possibilities. These possibilities were not open to other ranks. The officers mess was considered the only place where the ladies could be accommodated safely. As for the other ranks they should observe a modest dress code until the ladies had left.

Sam and Scouse, now in flippers, pushed through the hot water of the shallows then lay back into the cooler water and kicked out for the raft. Early on Sam had discovered that just plain swimming was a bit boring; boring and strenuous. Lionel had equipped himself with mask, snorkel and flippers starting a craze which had seen the Naafi shop run out of snorkels in no time. Sam wasn't much good with the snorkel and after a few choking incidents had abandoned it in favour of holding his breath. The effortless speed achieved with the flippers made this easier. A square of plywood acted as a hydroplane enabling a sort of underwater flying to be performed. Scouse had discovered that he could lay on his back with the board under his shoulders and plane his way across the lagoon. The whole business of swimming became much more fun.

Hauling themselves up onto the raft they sat with their feet in the water; the sun warm on their backs, the matting comfortable under their bare bums.

'Brilliant bomb. Poor old Yorkie'll be right cheesed off, it being a Valiant that did the dropping.' Scouse screwed his eyes up and scanned the beach. 'D'you reckon we can write home about it?'

Sam wondered. What would Grace make of his description of listening to Jazz and being warmed and buffeted by a big megaton hydrogen bomb.

'Who would you write to?' he asked the Liverpudlean.

'Me mam; she'd be fair chuffed to hear about it, it'd be round our street in no time. There's some Eyeties live at the bottom; can't remember any spies though.'

'You could tell her to keep it to herself...'

Scouse blew his cheeks out and laughed.

'Do I look like King fucking Canute! She'd tell everyone just the same but get them to keep it to themselves. It'd be in Moscow by tea time.'

'I reckon the Russians probably know all about it anyhow,' Sam pondered, 'let them know what's in store for them.

'Girl friends would be more dangerous.'

'What more dangerous than your mum?'

'I know me mam; she'd get the whole thing bolloxed up. With clever girls you're never sure. Get some lovely female spy find out I'm on Christmas Island and I'd be quids in'. He paused, thinking about the lovely spy, then asked,

'Did you get that Trowbridge bird's address?'

'The little blonde, Jill?' Sam thought back to that last

evening in Erlestoke.

Christine

Dancing

Erlestoke was grey, the days were long and money was short. On Friday evening Sam and the gang would set off for Trowbridge. A coffee bar and assorted pubs made for an evening of mild excitement. On Friday evenings there was a hop. The bus ride passed through an eternity of farming country before reaching the town. Once off the bus they headed for the Crown which looked out onto a square and across to the Assembly rooms. Cuthbert specials were the thing. Lager and blackcurrant with a vodka.

'Why Cuthbert?' new arrivals asked.

'Bill Cuthbert,' they were told. 'The inventor of the cocktail. He perfected it after many experiments. Got just the right blend of thirst slaking beer with a small amount of added alcohol and then the black currant to give a sense of enjoyable frivolity to the scene.'

'Is Cuthbert still with us?' they would ask.

'In spirit only,' would be the reply to whoops of laughter. The truth was nobody could remember where the Cuthbert special had come from. The point was it could get you loose enough to ask a girl to dance in no time at all.

The last Sunday evening before embarking for the island they had gone into town and toured the old haunts. At the end of the evening Sam and the others had landed up in the coffee bar. The bunch of girls were there including the little blonde. The gorgeous little blonde. Sam had that terrible affliction; she was so beautiful he couldn't speak to her. The banter had continued and eventually it had come time to catch the last bus.

'You lads going then?' A dark haired girl with heavy lipstick and looped earrings had asked. 'Give me a walk home if you are.' She gathered her bag and cigarettes from the table and said good night to the other girls. Sam watched the blonde and for a brief moment their eyes met. She was beautiful. He desperately wanted to speak to her but... the last bus and...

The dark haired girl pushed herself against him linking her arm through his. 'You'll walk me home, won't cha?' and suddenly he was walking beside this girl a long way behind Sid, Scouse and Robbie and then he was heading off down a side street and being squeezed into an alley way. She pushed her mouth against his and, being twenty, he pushed his mouth against hers. They kissed for a long time. She was soft with large breasts. She knew where to feel, what to do, and Sam responded.

They wove their way through the backstreets and suddenly they were in country side. She opened a gate and they entered a barn. This was some kind of dream, Sam thought. Barns and hay. They rolled down and got on with the business of finding condoms and the exquisite pleasure of putting one on. They made love with a hunger that only twenty year olds have. Despite all the bravado, all the stories, this sort of thing was incredibly rare in Sam's life.

They settled back into the hay and lit cigarettes. She was talkative.

'Christine,' she introduced herself.

'Sam,'

'I just came back from London,' she explained. 'Been up to see my gran for the weekend. Thought I'd look in at the Casbah and sure enough the gang's all there and you lot.' She dragged on her cigarette. 'Lucky that eh?' She reached down and gave him a squeeze where it mattered. 'You lot are off abroad tomorrow so I hear.'

'How'd you know that,' Sam wondered.

'All the local lads know it,' she continued, 'can't wait for you lot to leave the field. We're all theirs then, no competition from you Londoners and Scousers n' that.'

'I can't be your boyfriend, not with us leaving on Tuesday.' Sam explained that tomorrow was confined to camp day with all the final preparations being seen to.

'I know that, silly,' she said. 'I just thought I would try my luck. You were there and I figured you'd be all right.'

'You fancied me then?'

'Well...' she paused, 'enough. Not as much as Jill mind you, she nearly faints every time she sees you. You'd be married now if she had her way.'

'Who's Jill? Sam asked.

'Little blonde girl. She was there tonight. Didn't you see her looking at you?'

Back on the raft Sam remembered the shock of hearing that Jill - now he knew her name - had fancied him. The sun beat down on the silent pair. Scouse nudged him.

'Did you, get her address?'

'No mate, I didn't.'

The Police station

Sam wondered about that night. For the first time in his life he began to appreciate how the tiniest things can make the biggest changes. The rest of the story had been equally astounding for by the time he and Christine had exhausted themselves it was near one thirty. He had found his way back into town feeling the early March cold in the night air. Perhaps the local police station would be a good place to start looking for a way back to camp.

'Got a lift and fell asleep. The bloke dropped me here,' he explained to the policeman on duty, a weary desk sergeant sipping a cup of tea beneath a fluorescent tube.

The phone rang and the sergeant answered it. Sam could hear the squeak of the woman's voice on the other end, loud in the quiet hallway.

'...and she's Ok then?' The policeman nodded as the other person spoke. 'I'll send a man round in the morning. Find out what happened... yes. Goodnight.'

He put the phone down. 'Some girl reported missing. Supposed to have left her grandmother's at about six and not showed up home 'til now. We'll have to find out what happened to her tomorrow. Her mum's been phoning since midnight and now she says the girl's too knackered to talk.

The conversation sent a chill up Sam's spine.

'Now then; about you. You say you got a lift. Where was that from then?'

'London,' said Sam.

'And he dropped you here? Must've gone right past Erlestoke. What's your name?'

In a time when very few people of Sam's age owned a car the local geography of strange counties like Wiltshire was a mystery. Where Erlestoke was compared with Devises was uncertain. Relative to the rest of Britain, totally beyond Sam. The bus driver knew; that was enough.

'I was asleep. Next thing I knew he said this was Trowbridge. I'm from the camp at Erlestoke. I thought you might have a police car going that way.'

The desk sergeant smiled. 'Why would I have a police car standing by?'

'In case of an emergency?' Sam hazarded.

'In Erlestoke! I'll turn Jim out: taxi. Got any money?'

Sam searched his pockets and managed to scrape together three pounds ten and some loose change.

'That should do it,' the sergeant said. 'You lot are off abroad on Tuesday, so I hear.' He dialled and waited, writing something on the pad in front of him.

'I reckon she'll have gone off with some lad when she got off the train... Oh hello Jim. You OK for a fare, town to Erlestoke? Three quid?' Squaddie, lost his way coming back to camp. OK.'

'He'll be round in quarter of an hour. Yeah,' he continued,' she'll 'ave got shacked up with some bloke. We can call round and have a chat with her after tea tomorrow. See what she'd been up to till this late .'

'But if she's all right now...' Sam began.

'We never take that for granted in the force. She might be frightened to speak out about something terrible. She could have been forced against her will into unspeakable acts. No; we always check. Did you tell this bloke you wanted Erlestoke?'

Sam was tired. Not at his quickest. 'I think I did. I may have said Trowbridge; you know how it is. As long as he's going nearer to where you want to be...'

'Of course.' the sergeant wrote on the pad. The silence gathered.

'I may have just mentioned we were near Devises.'

'Oh, he'd have known Devises. Big place. County town really.'

The door pushed open and big grey haired man in a tweed coat pushed his way in.

'Hello Jim. This is the lad.'

'Right, Erlestoke is it. Three quid.' Sam handed over the money. 'OK then, I'll see you later Bert,' he said to the desk sergeant.

'You're all right for finding Erlestoke, Jim?' asked the policeman. 'Not many people have even heard of it have they. He smiled. 'You take care lad,' he nodded toward Sam. 'I expect your girl friend'll be OK. See you Jim.'

Back on the raft Scouse gave a shout. 'Hey! Jeezus! Some buggers lost some tropical fish! Look!'

Sure enough a shoal of tiny guppies swam around their feet. Sam laughed.

'Scouse, we are in the middle of the Pacific ocean. We're the ones who are lost.'

Family Thoughts

Family

Scouse had appeared when Sam went for his trade training in Chatham. In army terms they went back a long way. Sitting on the raft in the lagoon Sam suddenly realised that he knew very little of the man. Of the soldier, yes.

'What about you?' he asked. 'I've never heard you talking about a girl friend.'

'Too chubby,' he pinched his tummy, 'thin buggers like you get all the birds. Anyway, I wouldn't want a girlfriend while I'm out here. I be worryin' all the time that she'd be off with some lad in a drape jacket while I'm pratting about in OG's. Huyton's full of teds. They mop up all the birds. There's guys getting dear Johns already and we've only been here five minutes. Doesn't take a girl long to figure a year is a while.

Sam hitched himself down into the warm lagoon and began to circle the raft swimming on his back and watching the Liverpudlean. His ciggy's were on the beach; maybe a waterproof pack would be the thing with a lighter. He swam on lazily.

The men that surrounded him, Sid, Robbie, Scouse and the others were the nearest thing to family that he had now. Mum was dead, dad had died in fifty five leaving Grace, his step mother. She regarded him as a disappointment. Maybe he regarded her as a disappointment. He could make no opinion about this: he had no experience to call upon. Other kids grew up in a family home based in one place. Sam had got off to a good start or so he guessed, then Adolf Hitler had butted in and Dad had gone to war in the Royal Engineers.

East Hill, where Mum and John - he didn't get called Sam until school - sheltered from the blitz, looked out North, down into the valley of the Thames. London lay like a grey jumble beyond the back window of number fifty six. He and Mum would watch the buzz bombs as they spluttered toward the centre of the capital. Would they get Earls Court? It's prominent domed roof was the only recognisable building in the greyness.

The Anderson shelter in the back garden was water logged almost as soon as it was finished and so the big dining room table became their refuge from the German bombs which fell nightly, their thumps and wails strangely synchronised to the dancing flames from the fireplace. After the war Mum had died. John/Sam went into a home and then, a bit later, into a Convent at Burgess Hill in Sussex; Saint Joseph's.

Mum's sister Jean would come down to the convent and take him to visit Brighton for the day. Dressed in her WREN's uniform. With her scarlet lipstick she represented all that was glamorous in the black and white world of the convent. Dad would come sometimes and take him on the speed boat. It was called Miss Julie, red and shiny with a growling roar of power that could be heard from the beach all day.

Sam kicked the flippers and remembered the rushing wake of the red boat as it hurtled across the space between the piers.

Dad had married Grace and brought Sam home to Tooting, a terrace house with a big bowl of fruit on the table.

'Like a Maharaja's palace!' Sam had said and then settled into the humdrum world of school and Sunday mornings perched on the cross bar of Dad's bike, scared witless as they hurtled down Church Lane to St Boniface's for Sunday Mass.

None of it planned or structured; he was keeping his head above water in a vast river that flowed slowly on from one experience to the next. Just as he did now, swimming aimlessly around the diving raft. He didn't want to be in the army, he didn't even want to be on a desert island and yet outside of all that... what?

'Time for a ciggy,' Scouse called and slid into the lagoon. They flippered their way back to the beach and a State Express.

Night duty

There are no seasons in the middle of the Pacific. Sunshine reigns day after day; relentlessly.

The toil of building roads suddenly ended and Sam was put on night duty.

Sergeant Hogarth was the man in charge of the 'scientific waterworks'.

'These,' he explained, 'are the most advanced water filtration systems known to man. We don't purify this water for drinking, we go way beyond that and purify it for developing films.' Sam and Geordie Thompson stood in a square concrete building with no doors in the doorways. The room functioned only as a shelter for the wall. Maybe twelve high by fifteen feet long this wall was covered in pipes and valves. All carefully colour coded in blue and red and green with arrows indicating direction of flow and dials indicating pressure and speed. It made no noise but the dials shivered as they monitored it's mysteries.

'Basically you have nothing to do but keep an eye on it and carry out any instructions that may come to you from this phone,' The sergeant indicated a black Bakelite phone that stood ominously silent on a small concrete pillar in the centre of the floor.

'What happens if we turn the wrong valve, does it blow up?' Geordie asked a broad grin on his face

'I will say only one thing. You will be in the shit for the rest of your days. It is a very simple system. Just make sure it does what it's doing now for as long as you are on shift.'

Both men noticed that the pipes and dials were doing nothing. Pressures were being registered and a sensation of water moving could only be imagined, it's sound perhaps mistaken for the breeze that blew through the doorway. The sergeant left and Harrison, who was the shift man on duty, took over.

'Piece of piss. I get though a book a week on this. Make sure you keep the sand swept out and don't drop any food on the floor. Ants and Bombay runners will be out like a shot. Bring a blanket and a pillow, this chair is a killer and it gets cold around three in the morning.'

And so water purification duties started. Sam would get an early call at half past one in the morning then traipse over to the guardroom and fill his flask. Walk the quarter mile picking his way through the palms by the light of his torch to the square concrete building and take over from Geordie.

'All right?'

'Yeah,' he would sign the log and Geordie would stumble off into the night his torch flickering among the palm trees.

Sam took a blanket which he wrapped around himself as the night wore on. The pipes would think; a soundless presence and the phone would sit silently on it's pedestal.

After a couple of hours he would sweep the floor clear of sand and do an inspection of all the dials. What he was looking for he had not the faintest idea. 'Difference,' Harrison had said, 'Anything changes ring nine.' Nothing changed. He read the figures from the diagram and pressed the alarm test button. The shrill beep would echo around the concrete walls and he would return to his book.

Sam swore you could read by the light of the milky way. It arched, vast, across the night sky and glittered with the cold malevolence of a reptilian eye down upon Sam as he tried to prove his point with a book. He knew little of astronomy; how close or far the stars he could see were. Light years they talked about. He wondered if the flashes from the bomb test were speeding out toward the pale, glittering arch. Was some other Sam sitting on some other planet with a book and a longing to be somewhere else. Somewhere with a Mum and a Dad. And a cat. He suddenly remembered Puddles his cat when he had been very young. A doodle bug had killed him when it blew the windows of their house out in East Hill.

The light began to gather outside the concrete room, seeping into the gloom beneath the trees. Beyond the path the land crabs rustled through the fallen, dry palm leaves. Sam's thoughts went back to that first day, leaning against the rough grey trunk of a tree and seeing one of these creatures for the first time.

'Why were they 'land' crabs,' he thought. Lionel reckoned that they had found more to eat on land; birds eggs, insects, mice. It seemed to Sam that the sea surrounding the island was teeming with life of one sort or another. Joe, a Gilbertese islander had shown Sam how to catch an octopus with a wire coat hanger.

'Twist, now!' Joe had shouted, his grin broad despite Sam's clumsiness. 'Haul him out, he will hang on. Sam pulled the little white octopus out. Only about six inches across, the tentacles of the soft little animal writhed on the wire its arms spiralling to grip Sam's finger. He gently slide the creature off the wire.

Joe laughed. 'You too soft to be an islander. You starve in a week!'

He was right. Fish came in batter with chips and vinegar. The octopus retreated into a crevice in the coral. The sea washed around their legs.

'First time he seen a London man,' said Joe.

'First time I seen an octopus,' said Sam, 'still at least we said hello.'

Joe and he had worked their way back to the beach through the clear, shallow water while the Pacific waves thundered against the reef fifty yards behind them.

Joe was amazing. Dark brown, shiny as a conker, his hair jet black and shining, his eyes always laughing.

'Got a smile like a grand piano!' Tommy Marks had said.

Joe came with other islanders to harvest the coconuts, the husks were used for making rope and matting. They also got to earn some cash working for the army. Bare footed they would clamber over crushed coral. Glass sharp it could cut deeply and yet their feet were like leather.

'Tough as old boots,' Tommy Marks had a simile for everything.

'Cept they don't need no boots,' Yorkie Carr observed back.

The light thickened. An hour of shift left.

Now Sam the Londoner, had met the South Sea Islander, a character as much a part of Sam's past as giant octopuses were, at least in literature and films. Man Friday from Robinson Crusoe, Joe could have played the part a treat; Joe was, after all Man Friday teaching the Londoner how to catch fish.

Benny was another product of the south seas, a Fijian on the island with the Fiji Regiment. Big lads, bigger than the small, wiry, Gilbertese. Smart in their uniforms which featured a skirt; not that anyone remarked upon it. Big lads the Fijians.

'The octopus and the Londoner,' he thought, 'not a lot of difference in the Gilbertese and the Londoner, or the Fijian and the Londoner. Sid had remarked that Sam always knew blokes who were bigger than him. Reckoned that it was a sort of protective strategy. Tommy Marks pointed out that at five six most of the rest of the world was bigger than Sam.

'Except Yorkie Carr and Louis Patchitti,' said Sam in his defence.

Benny and Sam got on well. Both played the guitar, Benny well, Sam getting better. The big Fijian showed him how to use shark line to string the guitar.

'Hun'red pount for de bass two, E an' A,'

'Pount?' Sam had queried.

'Pounds,' Louis Patchitti explained.

'Pount, what I said,' Benny looked puzzled that these Brits couldn't understand their own language. He shook his head and continued.

'den sempty pount for middle two, D an' G, fifty pount for top two, B an' E. Listen this'. He had played the nearest thing to slide guitar without a slide that Sam had ever heard. The nylon line was smooth, not wire wound like real guitar strings, and so there was no squeaking as his fingers slid from one note to the next. The chords slid into one another shifting seamlessly - glissandi Sam learnt twenty years on - then Benny would sing, a great shouted sound that challenged the constancy of the trade wind. Two others joined him each straining their big black arms around to play two stings of the guitar and each shouting his own part in this Pacific ocean harmony. Maybe he was just being soft, maybe he had seen too many films about the south seas but Sam could see long, outrigged war canoes as the music spread into the warm night.

Harrison arrived. 'OK?' he said signing in on the log.
'Yeah.'
Sam walked slowly back to camp for breakfast and bed.

CHAPTER 6

Sleeping

Silence

  The only problem with night duty was the sleeping. Bunking down at half past eight in the morning was not really the best time to try to sleep. The camp, although half empty with most working, still resonated to the new day. At ten the truck would turn up to empty the Elsans; a task that most avoided talking about. The RAF regiment guys got a big bonus for doing this job. Such was the nature of the task that few envied them their bonus. The other interruptions included anyone coming back to the tent for something always wanted to chat, oblivious to the fact that Sam had been up all night. Lunch time would bring an influx of men anxious for a post prandial nap. The sound of them flopping out woke Sam most days. Unfairly they would then drop off for half an hour before stirring again to continue the day.

  As the shifts rotated so Sam would come back to the four o'clock shift. Finishing at twelve this gave the best night's sleep.

  Tommy Marks brought the subject of women up.

  'Nearly three months since I last saw a bird. I reckon if I go on at this rate I could forget what a woman looks like.'

  'You see plenty of women in the films.' said Lionel.

  'If I'd ever seen a woman looks like one of them I'd desert and marry her.'

  'A woman like that Liz Taylor or Marilyn Monroe wouldn't look twice at a bloke like you,' Scouse chipped in.

  'Anyway,' Yorkie Carr piped up, 'they're not really real, are they. All painted up and dressed to the nines. Not real women like you meet at home.'

  Sam remembered Christine. Her full softness almost made his mouth water. 'Just like roast lamb with mint sauce,' he mused. How odd that the senses got mixed up with the absence of girls; making him think of food! Four and a half thousand men on a desert island. The stories went about that the queers thought they were in heaven. 'Poufter's Paradise,' some called it.

They were only stories though. Most of Sam's experience was hazy here. When he had first joined up as a boy soldier he knew that some of the older lads had raped the new recruits; had heard it in the darkness after lights out when twenty odd boys had feigned sleep while one of their number was used to pleasure two older boys. No one had ever approached him and so he had, like all the rest, kept quiet; remained unseeing, unhearing. Perhaps uncomforting to the lad who wept after they had finished.

For now he was just happy to be on the evening shift. Less pressure to drink and perhaps more time to dream of Christine and Jill.

Dream

With sleep came dreaming.

'You lads going then?' The dark haired girl with heavy lipstick and looped earrings asked. 'Give me a walk home if you are.' Sam now watched while she took Sid's arm, watched and trailed behind then turned on the wet pavement and walked back toward the coffee bar. The little blonde came out, alone and walked towards him. He wanted to speak but the words and pictures had missed the gears like a movie when the film jumps from the sprockets and the images dance on the screen.

She waited and the silence grew, became bigger somehow filling the whole world as he looked at her beautiful face. Her blonde hair swept up Audrey Hepburn style, held with a black velvet ribbon. Her blue eyes wide in the darkness and... only silence.

Sam woke into the thick blackness of the tent. The darkness was still, the silence of his dream continuing. He grew more awake, more aware. No flapping. The silence was real. No heaving of the canvas in the warm air. The wind had dropped for the first time in months. Then, very gently, it began to rain.

Rain

Eventually the rain woke them all up. A match flared. 'Pissing down,' Scouse voiced the obvious in the darkness and his cigarette ember glowed fiercely in the gloom.

'Reveille in ten minutes, bloody hell, switch the light on.'

Sam, not on duty until eight, felt swindled out of his extra hour. Nothing for it but to get going. The rain was freezing. He supposed it was really quite warm but after his time on the island he was used to warm, balmy air.

Scouse spat tooth paste out, cursed and ran back to the tent. The light grew stronger revealing an island that was almost strange to them.

'Like fucking Liverpool on a Monday morning,' he said as they wiped themselves dry.

'Why Monday?' Sam asked.

'Worst day of the week. Worst day to have off because it just becomes a bit of the weekend. Worst day of the week to be at work, every other bugger hates it so they all take it out on each other. Worst day of the week to be sick, the quack is snowed under because people just don't want to go to work and there's you at deaths' door while all these skiving sods use up the sick chit allocation. Worst day to be happy 'cos every other bugger is miserable. Hates Mondays.'

'Wednesday today.' Tommy Marks fumbled a newspaper from his bedside box and folded it in four.

'Umbrella.' he explained and set off for breakfast.

'What happened to the wind?' Yorkie Carr plonked his tray on the table.

'Becalmed,' said Lionel, 'the ancient traders hated this. Days spent drifting aimlessly...'

'Not much sailing to do then?' Tommy Marks joined in.

'It wasn't that. They only had a limited amount of water and food. Going nowhere and still using water could be a disaster.'

'So are we in the doldrums then?'

'No, they occur in a definite area. This is becalmed. Could last for days nobody knows.'

'We ought to go sailing,' said Tommy.

'What, you mean sail home?' Sam wondered, only two thousand miles to Hawaii and that was a million miles from the mouth of the Thames.

'Twat! No. I know where there's a boat. We could sail about in the lagoons one day. It's only a folding assault craft. We'd have to row.'

'Pissing with rain and Marks reckons we should go sailing, Jesus!' Scouse drained his mug and headed for work.

CHAPTER 7

Tests again

Another Test 28th April 1958

Another test. Another morning squatting on the sand grass listening to Jazz, watching for the vapour trails, unscrewing thermos flasks.

Pete Cunningham, who had seen it all before said, 'If you screw your fists up like you were pretending to use a pair of binoculars,' he demonstrated, ' only instead of leaving a big hole to look through leave only a tiny hole and make sure you look down at the ground in front of you, then you can see the flash.'

'That why you wear glasses Pete?' Scouse asked.

'You've tried this?' Sam asked.

'Yeah. It's weird. All the shadows disappear. No shadows, no shapes so really you can't see anything, just white. You should try it'

Pete began to clean his glasses as if in readiness. The white patch at the top of his nose, where the bridge had been, wrinkled as he polished the lenses. His eyes looked unusually weak without their normal framework.

'Yeah,' said Sam.

'You going to have a go then?' Sid screwed his big hands into fists and twisted them as if adjusting the focus.

'Yeah.' Sam squinted through his 'fist bino's' looking down at the coarse grass that grew through the coral sand. He remembered Montrose.

Montrose

Dad had called it sand grass. Razor sharp blue green grass that cut you if you were not careful with it. They sat among the dunes that lay above Montrose beach Sam being dried in the rough white towel, shivering as his father rubbed some warmth back into his thin white body. They had been plunging. Dad had reasoned that if you could swim under water and surface when you wanted to then you would learn to swim on the surface without the fear of submerging. Sam would stand with the water up to his armpits then leap and plunge like a dolphin and swim with his eyes open, just above the ridged sand. His father's legs, planted astride like two massive pillars, lay ahead for him to swim between then he would surface; blowing out, breathing in, blowing out. Brilliant.

The lesson finished they had waded ashore hugging themselves against the breeze that blew along the golden beach from the North. As they started up the hard sand Sam had trodden on a jelly fish half buried in the sand; maybe a foot and a half across, the soft cold giving of the flesh made him shriek, a long high pitched scream that vied with the wind and waves to be heard. Dad had whisked him up, holding him tight as they both stared down at the creature, dead and dull like an old man's eye. Dad told him it was dead, told him that the stingers were underneath then rubbed his stubbled chin against his son's cheek to make all well. Sam was eight.

On top of the dunes, in the sea grass they looked out to Scudie Ness, the point with it's lighthouse that bounded the shallow bay to the South. Scotland; cold with bright sun, deserted beaches, sand dunes and behind them golf links stretching to the railway. They would dress and hurry to the level crossing. Dad would smoke a cigarette while they waited for 'The Bervie Express'.

Scotland was railway. Hauled from London by the Flying Scotsman. They would arrive at the station and settle step mum Grace into a window seat with the luggage then Dad would take Sam to see the engine. Once, he had been lifted onto the footplate and had been allowed to pull down the regulator lever moving the engine - as yet uncoupled - gently forward. Then down to watch the couplings being hauled over the hooks and the hoses connected. Back to the carriage and off. After about half an hour the travel sickness would take hold and last on and off until sleep liberated him from the dry retching.

The Bervie Express hooted in the distance and Dad leaned on the top bar of the crossing gate while Sam climbed onto the white cross bar. The small engine came into sight, three carriages rattling behind. The driver and stoker would wave and steam would swirl about as the wave of heat from the fire box and boiler rolled over them.

The warmth passed up Sam's back now as he clenched his fists to his eyes but this time looked through the tiny hole to see the course coral sand and grass vanish into a shadowless brightness that threatened to blind. He felt the warmth and heard again the long high pitched scream from the Scottish beach and closed his eyes tightly.

Sailing

The usual procession back to camp and then sit around watching the big mushroom cloud change from a man made monstrosity into high natural looking cloud that sought to blend itself into the Pacific sky as if ashamed of its origin.

The chat turned to sailing. Tommy figured they could get some supplies together and explore the lagoons that led out to the sailing club.

'Funny,' thought Sam, 'it must be something about desert islands that make people want to sail off them.' He supposed that if you were a castaway, either shipwrecked or abandoned for being a pain in the arse to the rest of the crew, you would naturally think about making for home. Later, in the Naafi, he had asked Benny about island hopping.

'You godda be good,' the big Fijian sipped orange juice and smoked a small cheroot. 'De reef is de fust of you' troubles. Big tides an' small tides is the time to hold back. In between tides is the time to go... ' he made a diving gesture with his open palm.

'Plus you need men: big long boat in waves is like being hit with a telephone pole. Man on the prow for weight and with a paddle to fend and dip, keepin' the front pointing out. Men at the back, each side pushing 'gainst the ocean, looking for the gully where da reef is broke. Big wave come in filling the lagoon then push, push, push as the water rushes back out an' go right through that next wave like a spear through soft fish. Run, jump, paddle. Run, jump, paddle; each man does this, never stopping, strain you' muscles real hard. Then you' there. Out on the big swell that tell you land is close then quiet and quiet,' he fluttered his hand gently, 'bail out the water that has come in. You are on the ocean. Follow the sun then follow the cross in the big arch of stars in the night. Sing, tell stories.' He closed his eyes tilting his head back. 'That was in my granddaddies day of course. Right now we get on a boat in da harbour.' He laughed his big broad laugh and drew hard on the cheroot.

'My granddaddy once ate human flesh d'you know?' Sam started at this.

'Was he a cannibal?'

'I guess so. Happen that he liked to tell us kids all sorts of stuff so you never did know. I asked him what it tasted like an' he said 'Chicken,' Chicken!' again the big broad laugh, 'every ting you pretend to have eat tastes like chicken!'

The expedition was planned in the usual haphazard way. Cold sausages from the Naafi, two boxes of beer. Plenty of cigarettes. Yeah, they could travel the world. Sam, Tommy, Yorkie Carr Scouse, Geordie Thompson and Mickey Doyle. They loaded themselves and the supplies into a dumper truck bucket and set off, jolting and whooping, for the hiding place of the boat. Tommy drove the truck.

'You tip this bucket and you're dead!' Sam shouted. Not really the place to travel, in a dumper truck bucket. Tommy heeded the warning. They arrived and Tommy parked the machine next to a ruined native hut. The boat lay collapsed like a flattened Cornish Pasty beneath the rotting hut roof.

These assault craft were a relic of the war. Built of plywood and canvas with a transom to take an outboard, they erected it by lifting the sides which then hauled the bow and the stern up so that it looked more like a giant seed pod than anything else Sam could imagine. They hauled it up onto the dumper bucket and Tommy drove gently to the shoreline of the deserted lagoon. Four oars were strapped to the sides.

'Probably sink,' thought Sam as the ancient ply wood flexed for the first time in ages.

'So no sailing then Tommy,' The question was general

'You can row, can't ya! Good enough for Cleo fucking patra, good enough for me.'

Once erected into a proper boat shape they pushed it into the warm water of the shallows. There was a good deal of rocking and splashing. Boats are hard to get in once they are floating; they either settle back down onto the bottom, skid away or threaten to capsize.

'Sam, grab hold of the side and hang on.' Tommy took charge. His boat so he's captain. Sam hung on while the rest clambered into the other side. Then he pushed off and hoisted himself in. It floated.

'Which way?'

'West,' said Tommy.

'England's North,' Yorkie Carr slotted an oar together and began to paddle as if heading for Yorkshire.

'What, on cold sausages and beer. We go north we're back on the beach. West you twat.' Tommy's boat.

They set off toward the opening where the lagoon met the next lagoon. Sam had no idea which direction they were headed and suspected that Tommy was just heading for open water knowing that the sailing club was that way. They finally got the rowing sorted and began to make good progress.

The gentle movement of the boat brought back memories of the raft on the canal in Aldershot. He tried to remember the lads involved, Gilly Gilbert, Chick Henman, Smiffy from Norfolk. Great lads, the first blokes he had known in the army. They had all started together, fifteen year olds herded into a red brick Victorian barracks from where they had bundled their civilian clothes up and sent them home. A one way ticket then; no civvies. No going back; you became a boy soldier. As for Sam, he acquired a family.

Not long after that the army had staged an open day at the place and a pensioner had told Sam the barracks had been condemned when he was a young soldier! Not surprising. The red brick of the place had an oldness about it. Door jambs had been warn smooth, painted, repainted maybe hundreds of times. Dark green. The floor boards broad and polished, again the dip of wear as you approached the doorway. Polished with a heavy bumper. Eventually the army must have realised it was going to fall down and so Gibraltar barracks had been closed and the boy soldiers moved into Malta barracks. Wooden huts on stilts; Sam never found out why stilts.

His memory of the camp - set in scrubby woodland - had been mostly of summer although he remembered walking on the frozen canal and sliding maybe twenty yards on the creaking ice. Mainly though it was always hot and sunny, surrounded by birch tree woods that provided a hunting ground for bored, penniless teenagers. The Basingstoke canal ran close by, the Mississippi for their Tom Sawyer adventures. Here he had learned to run.

To get out of games you became a runner so Sam, who hated games took up running. He had found he was good at it, had also found that when you ran you could think. Think like no other time. The steady pace, the regular breathing, the familiar route all served to calm him down, all served to let his mind wander and wonder at this freedom.

During that time, October fifty four, boy sergeant Beaman had handed him the Daily Mirror.

'Anything to do with you,' he said, pointing to a headline about a male nurse called Alan Smart who had died after being kicked by a lunatic. The address was nearly right and St John's in East hill was where Dad worked. Beaman took him to the guard room and summoned the orderly officer. Enquires were made. Sam's Dad was dead.

He ran on, steady pacing, steady breathing, alone on the road.

The boat grounded.

'Bloody hell!' Tommy Marks stabbed his oar over the side hitting coral and sand.

'What do we do now?' Scouse opened a beer.

'Good idea,' Geordie Thompson opened a beer. The sun beat down and Yorkie started on the cold sausages.

'If we eat all the food perhaps it'll refloat,' Yorkie pushed his glasses up and chomped a bit more sausage.

'You'd have to crap over the side to make that work and I'm buggered if I'm sittin' here watchin' you lighten your load.' Mickey Doyle grinned, 'we could get out and push, it'd float without us in.'

'Brilliant,' Tommy opened a beer, 'have this first then get out and piss. Belt and braces. Brilliant.'

And so they got out and started to push.

'Anyone seen the picture, 'The African Queen?' Mickey related the highlights as they pushed. Sam could feel the finger coral through his plimsolls. Sharp stuff but the boat moved easily enough. They sweated for ages then the water began to get deep again. Old hands now they clambered back into the boat and began to row once more.

'Be nice if we had a sail,' Sam said.

'Be nice if we had some water,' said Scouse.

'There's a few cans left,' Said Tommy.

'I meant to sail the fucking boat in. You've got to remember yer talking to a lad raised on the Mersey! Big bloody river the Mersey'

'I wasn't so far from the Thames. What about you Sam must've been down to the Thames; best river in the world?' Tommy heaved on the oar.

'Yeah, me and doc Shaw used to bunk off school. Go up London and muck about near Tower bridge...'

'How'd you get up to the city then,' Tommy asked, 'you were down in Tooting, so you told me.'

'You could sneak under the ticket office at Clapham south which was nearest to our school then, when we got up to Waterloo or London bridge you mucked about on the escalators until a porter came along and threw you out.'

'Didn't they ever figure that out then,' Mickey Doyle took over Yorkie's oar. 'Recognise you from another time like?'

'I don't know. I don't think they gave a toss really. Kids just got ordered around. You told them what to do and they did it, we never made decisions or acted responsibly, we just presented a bloody nuisance to be moved on. Sometimes we would get a platform ticket and take a train to Hampton Court and muck about on the river'.

'How'd you get out of the station then?'

'Back down the track and climb under the bridge that went over the Mole. We used to put pennies on the line and get them flattened by the next train.'

'Exciting life, mate.' Tommy lit a fag and smiled up into the sun. It was bloody hot work rowing.

The River

The river had featured big in Sam's life. Looking back he remembered reading 'Three men in a Boat'. The first book he had really read; the first book to make him laugh out loud while he was reading. The sensation of laughing at something written all that time ago still fascinated him. He had canoed on the river in his own canoe, a collapsible Tyne Craft, when he had been on leave from boys service thanks to Billy Bean, the quartermaster who had spotted their potential as a result of their rafting adventures.

'Right, this will be the canoe club.' Billy Bean, a jovial warrant officer, balding but with a feeling of strength in his baldness, had gathered them around on the first evening. He had produced plans. They had made frames of cheap wood. Sam tried to remember; maybe ten frames each slightly different in size to make the profile of a Kayak canoe.

'As used by the Eskimos of the north pole,' Billy had told them. They had chiselled and planed, glued, screwed and assembled the craft, each to hold a two man crew. Finally they had stretched canvas over the framework and then painted and painted it with gloss paint until Billy was satisfied that it would be waterproof. Sam now suspected that the paint was a little more than just domestic gloss.

The canoes had lasted well and the canoe club had become popular with trips to Guildford on the river Wey. Tinned stew boiled up in a square biscuit tin had gone down well while they had camped on some island or other. A big chunk of white bread to wipe the plate round...

Sam could taste it now as he sweated under the Pacific sun edging toward the line of palms, silver grey in the strong sunlight and beneath them the sailing club. The beer had all gone so the boat was lighter but now they were thirsty. The chunk of white bread he would trade a thousand times for a glass of water.

The Sailing Club

The club was a white stucco building that looked as if it had been imported direct from some Mediterranean beach resort. For the use of officers only. Typical. Squaddies had to make do with a dumper truck and the African Queen and officers got to have boats with sails and a white stucco club straight out of the films. They rowed towards it and grounded gently on the white beach in front of the place.

'We won't be allowed in there, dead cert,' said Geordie Thompson.

'You go in, Sam,' said Tommy, 'you've got the rabbit.'
'Rabbit?'
'Talk; rabbit and pork. Ask if we can have a drink out the water cooler'.

Sam climbed out of the boat and walked up to the building stepping onto a tiled floor; the most civilised floor he had walked on for months. Smooth, cool and firm; a million miles from concrete, sand and duckboards. Paper strip blinds shifted gently in the breeze and a man in whites sat in a wicker chair reading a newspaper.

'Good afternoon,' Sam said, unsure whether to add a Sir: the man wore no badges of rank.

'Hello,' said the man, folding his paper, 'where the devil did you spring from?'

'A sailing trip. From the main camp,' Sam hadn't really expected to be asked about the madcap expedition. 'we got a bit lost and we are a bit thirsty.'

'Bar's closed old chap. You could use the water cooler.' he indicated the machine in the corner of the hallway. 'How many of you?'

'Six.'

'Bloody hell,' he ran his hand through his dark hair, 'Well, I reckon we'll manage. Ration yourselves. What did you come in?

'An assault craft. We rowed.'

The man got up and went to the door. He eyed the beached craft with the five men leaning on its sides.

'Probably pushed it more than you rowed I would say. These shallow lagoons mark the sort of marshy area where the reef has broken. That's why we have the sailing club here; we can get out into the ocean without getting pounded by big waves breaking on a reef. Come on in then,' he shouted and Sam watched as the ragtag crew climbed out of the boat. This chap was obviously an officer. Knew a whole lot more about the island than anyone Sam had met. Broken reef. He would ask Benny about that.

They shuffled in and began to empty the water cooler. The officer arrived with a refill bottle and six cans of root beer.

'Three bob to you lot,' he said. They searched their pockets and came up with the money then took their leave and started back to the boat.

'How are you getting back?'

'Same way we came,' Sam could think of no other way; they had got to the edge of the island. Sea from now on. 'Could we sail round?'

'No, this is the only landing place apart from the port and you mustn't go on the sea in that thing. You wouldn't last five minutes. Go back the way you came. Best way I suppose. Have a good trip.' He stood on the beach, his feet planted firmly in the sand, his hands in the pockets of his white shorts, watching them get afloat once more. Sam waved once they were under way and the chap waved back.

'Nice bloke,' Tommy lit a fag.

'Yeah,' said Sam, 'I need a piss now.'

Back again

Sam peed and started a craze. The boat rocked and heaved as they took turns over the stern. Then they hit the shallow waters of the inner lagoon.

'Sod this, man,' Geordie Thompson threw his oar down, 'Why don't we row over there and ditch the boat. We're going to be walking a fair amount from now on. Bleedin' boat weighs a ton.'

'S'pose you're right,' Tommy scanned the shore. 'Over there,' he indicated a stretch of sand. They rowed over and landed.

'Pull the boat up under the trees and we can use it from here next time.'

'Where the fuck's here?' Jimmy Doyle wanted to know.

'We'll know when we get back to camp, won't we.' Tommy laughed. 'Could do with a walk after being cooped up on a boat all day. What's the time?'

'Quarter to four. Where's the dumper from here?' asked Sam.

'Can't be far,' Tommy helped hauling the boat up into the bending palms that fringed the shore. They stowed the oars and collapsed the craft down to its crushed Cornish pasty shape. Geordie and Mickey dragged palm fronds over it.

'Not too many, we'll never find it again.' Tommy took up his explorer pose. 'Round the edge of this lagoon and round the edge of the next one and there will be our dumper.

The fact that whilst striking an impressive pose the cockney explorer had missed one lagoon meant that they missed tea.

Scouse fretted until six thirty then set off for the Naafi and double burger and chips.

'Fucking hungry work this sailing,' he swigged his Tennants.

'When we going again?' asked Yorkie Carr.

'Same time next fucking year,' said Scouse, convincingly.

Sam wondered where he would be this time next year. Not on Christmas Island that was for sure.

CHAPTER 8

Hawaii

Holiday, hooray

'Ha fuckin' wyee, mate!' Some how it seemed the right pronunciation, complete with bad language, coming from Geordie Thompson.

'Smart, Thompson, Robinson, Doyle. You four are off to Hawaii Monday morning for two glorious weeks rest and recuperation.'

The announcement, delivered by sergeant Kent, a burly man with a broad smile, came as a complete surprise to Sam. He hadn't actually considered that leave was possible from the island it being in the middle of the biggest ocean in the world.

'Women, ' Mickey Doyle grinned his widest grin.

'Monday morning at eight the truck will take you to the airfield. Be in the cookhouse for seven to get your breakfast and rations for the journey. OK?'

'How long does it take to get to Hawaii then?' Sam posed the question being the most interested of the group when it came to being in an aeroplane for any length of time. He liked them, was thrilled about them but still remembered the orange on the way out.

'Six hours and no smoking!' the sergeant smiled, 'you'll have to puff a few before takeoff to see you through.'

'But we could smoke on the way out here, sarg, what's so special about this plane?' Robbie lit a cigarette as he spoke as if to start the stocking up process early.

'That was a civilian aircraft, you'll be in a raff Hastings the ones with the extra fuel tanks under the bogs so you can forget a crafty drag while you have a piss.'

Monday morning saw the four, along with men from other squadrons filing up the steps into the silver 'plane. Sam noticed that his rations contained an orange and decided to save it until he was firmly on the ground in Hawaii. Six hours of relentless ocean followed. No islands, no boats just glittering sea from horizon to horizon. Sam went to the toilet a couple of times but convinced himself he could smell petrol.

They touched down at Hickam field, a US air force base and filed into a customs shed where the customs officer confiscated the orange throwing it into a blue bin for incineration.

A raff sergeant read them the riot act. Sam's mind wandered as he looked over the American airfield. Different smells than the island. Different uniforms, sandy coloured and smart. Why were the British army outfits so bad? He joined the lecture as the sergeant mentioned that Hickam canteen would provide a breakfast if you showed your id card anytime up to nine in the morning and that they would be staying at the YMCA in Honolulu city.

'Some blokes get all the cushy jobs,' Mickey nodded toward the sergeant, 'posted to Honolulu and all we got was Erlestoke and Christmas Island. Bet this bloke's got three hula hula girls on the go!' He wiggled his hips and made hula girl hand movements. At five foot four and tubby the movement didn't quite come off.

'They'd have to stop hoolering for a bit.' Robbie laughed as they got onto the bus into town.

River Street

The YMCA in River Street Honolulu was an American building. Why it was an American building Sam could not say but the description took root in his imagination and so instead of walking into the reception area of the YMCA they walked into the foyer of a slightly seedy American hotel as seen in countless films.

'Well, near enough,' thought Sam.

The building was certainly old and certainly had the feel of rundown gentility about it with a reception desk which stretched down one side of the hallway. Leather settees lined the opposite wall.

'Hi,' the voice was followed by a head rising from behind the desk.

'Oh, right,' said Robbie, 'Thompson, Doyle, Smart and Robinson.'

'ID' The clerk thumbed the book open.

Sam fished his identity card from his shirt pocket and laid it on the desk with the others.

'Royal Engineers. Oh my! Yes Sir, you boys is more than welcome.' his dark-skinned face broke into a broad smile. 'Sign up here. You're in a pair of double rooms so how you share is up to you, Yes Sir, here's the keys, up one floor for your rooms, yes Sir!' The smile continued as they headed up the hall for the lift.

'What brought that on?' Geordie wondered'

'Royal', said Robbie, 'They really like that in America. We just take it for granted but they reckon the queen comes out and inspects us every morning. We are a class act according to them.'

'I wonder if they will start bowing,' Sam grinned at his own thought and bowed to them all as they filed out of the lift.

Two beds and a wardrobe, a desk with a hard chair and little else described the bland fustiness of the room. Robbie flopped onto the bed near the window and Sam contented himself with the remaining bed. The silence was complete, uncanny in some strange way. Sam realised that they had lived since March with the constant company of the trade wind fretting at the canvas of their marquee. A quiet room really was uncanny.

'Pete Cunningham told me that there is a bar up the street, fancy a pint?'

Sam agreed. He had no idea how to spend a holiday in Hawaii so a pint in the bar would be as good a place as any to begin this new adventure.

In Town

The bar on the corner was run by a Scotsman with a head of wild dark hair and a thin tanned face still with the stamp of Scottish pessimism even in the warmth of this Pacific island. It made asking questions easier. The four ordered drinks.

'My Dad was from Aberdeen,' Sam told the Scot.
'Glasgow me. Were you born there?'
'No, London,'
'Ach! someone's got to live there.' He polished a glass and the four of them quizzed him about the city.

'You'll be needing a woman if you've been on that island since March,' the Scotsman said', 'Try the massage parlours, they're best. It's illegal to tout from the pavement and anyone who does is a bit... you know.'

Sam wondered if he should know. The idea of going to a massage parlour for sex presented him with so many questions. Did you just ask? For what?

Robbie put him straight.

'Once you turn over onto your back mate the subject may just come up.' He bent his elbow in the well known signal.

'Jesus Christ,' Sam thought and took a long drink from his glass.

At the suggestion of the barman they took a bus into the centre of Honolulu.

This was a new experience. They paid the driver; no conductor! They asked for the town centre.

'Don't matter where you go,' the driver told them, 'one fare, thirty two cents. One stop or right to the end of the line, thirty two cents.'

The system seemed to Sam really efficient. No conductor traipsing about and everyone who got on paid the same fare so it was quick. The bus wove through the unfamiliar streets picking up passengers here and there then emerged into a wide road with tall hotel buildings between which Sam caught a sight of the sea.

'Here I reckon,' Mickey Doyle rang the bell and they got out to find Waikiki beach.

The Beach

The street was lined to the right with high hotel buildings. The view of the sea being caught between them and sometimes through them for often they seemed to stand on glass. Robbie pushed his way through a revolving door and they discovered the reasoning behind the layout. You got to the beach through the bar, or a shop. When you needed to get to the beach you were encouraged to part with some cash!

Robbie ordered the beers.

Sitting overlooking the beach Sam wondered at being in this place that had, up to this point, only existed in films. At the end of the bay lay the vast bulk of Diamond head, almost a mountain to anyone from London. People enjoyed the warm waves and dabbled about in the sand much as people all over the world behaved on a beach. The Scotsman had told them that the sand was imported because the sea kept washing it away. Hard to imagine.

'I'm going for a walk,' he said, 'have a think.'

'OK mate, we'll still be here for a while,' Robbie leaned back taking a long drink from his beer.

The sand was soft, the air seemed somehow warmer than Christmas island air, maybe just because the breeze was not that constant trade wind. Warmer and scented. He realised that he was smelling perfume; tan lotion, scent, things that were missing on the island because there were no women. Here seemed to be filled with women. To Sam's hungry eyes they all looked beautiful; they certainly smelled beautiful. Glamour. That was what he was seeing for the first time in months, real flesh and blood glamour.

His mind found the memory of Auntie Jean and the red speed boat at Brighton. They had whooped and been splashed as the roaring, red Miss Julie had thundered across the bay between the piers that reached out to the horizon. Jean had put her arm about his shoulders and he had smelled her perfume as he did now on this South Pacific beach. He squinted out at the sparkling ocean. Boats but no roaring Miss Julie. This was not the seaside. At home the seaside was speed boats and candy floss, sand castles with little windmills whirring in the breeze. This beach - he refused to call it seaside - was for adults with hotel bars serving drinks to tanned couples who read books and smoked cigarettes. Maybe the kids version was better. Sam walked on towards Diamond head which remained forever distant.

He joined Robbie and the others and they decided to explore the main street. Again the sense of somewhere entirely different tainted Sam's thoughts. Big cars 'All on the wrong side of the road!' according to Mickey, and now the smell of the traffic dominated. Hot food and perfume mingled with the noise of the street. Music.

'Yakety yak! yakety yak! The Coasters hit thumped out onto the pavement, lifting their spirits.

'Burger,' Geordie led them into a long cool cafe and they settled themselves around a table.

The waitress appeared, her blonde hair topped with a pretend mob cap. She placed glasses of water for each of them.

'And what would you boys like?' she produced a pencil from her hair and flipped a little pad from nowhere. Robbie grinned and Sam studied the menu. Unable to make much sense of what each dish would be like he decided on the burger.

'With relish sir?'

'Yes please...' he wondered whether to add a ma'am.

'You boys from England?' she continued.

'Yes...' again the ma'am hovered.

'I would just love to go to England and see your Queen and her sister. They are so, oh, you know, so classy.

'We're in the royal army,' Robbie broke into the conversation. He pulled out his ID card and held it for her to see. Sam thought he looked a bit like an FBI agent flashing his card prior to questioning.

She took the card held it up betraying her bad eyesight.

'And you boys are all engineers. Oh my. I guess you know her Rolls Royce just back to front and upside down.' She scribbled their orders onto her pad and left for the kitchen with a final 'oh my!'

'So now you're a royal car mechanic.' Mickey grinned at Robbie, 'be well in there if she's got a car in need of attention. Be good with a dipstick there!'

The food arrived. Big hamburger steaks with ringed onions laid on an open sesame bun. Around the outside of the dish a different relish in each of the dimpled recesses. They ordered coffee to help it down and ate in greedy silence for a while.

CHAPTER 9

The American way

Don't Walk

The holiday progressed. Geordie Thompson almost got himself arrested.

'What the fuck you up to man!' he protested as a policeman pushed him to face a wall and kicked at his feet to spread his legs.

'Caint read?' the policeman held his gun and pushed the butt between Geordie's shoulder blades. 'Don't walk says the sign, that mean you don't walk!'

Robbie risked butting in. 'We're new here. Didn't see the sign. I have an ID card.'

The policeman eyed Robbie.

'You from England?'

'That's right. Royal army. I can show you the card.'

Standing slightly apart Sam noted that Robbie had his hands up which, given the gun in the policeman's fist seemed a good idea. Robbie pointed to his top pocket. Being dressed only in a pair of shorts, flip flops and a gaudy Hawaiian shirt it would have seemed impossible to conceal a fire arm. The policeman nodded and Robbie produced his ID.

'OK,' he lifted his weight from between Geordie' shoulders and holstered his gun. 'You just have to remember t' use your eyes. Do what the sign says. Wait 'til it says 'walk' then you can cross the road.' He straightened his uniform shirt and turned Geordie away from the wall brushing the front of his rumpled shirt as if signing off the incident. 'You boys enjoy your stay.'

'Fucking jumpy lot,' Geordie said after the policeman had turned the corner, 'bastard would've shot me!'

'All these yanks carry guns,' said Mickey.

'They aren't Yanks,' said Robbie, 'not yet. They reckoned they were going to be the fiftieth state but Alaska beat them to it. These are Hawaiians. The guys with the sunglasses on and the big Harley Davison's are HASP's Hawaiian Armed Services Police. That guy was just Honolulu police department.'

'They've got two police forces. It's only a little island,' Sam wondered how Robbie knew all these things and asked.

'Same as Malta, little island easily overrun so you have the local police and a whole load of military who are kept in line with the military police talking of which...' Robbie nodded as two redcaps turned the corner.

'You lads behaving yourselves?' The burly military policeman looked menacing but Sam decided that it was only the sharply cut peak of his cap that gave him this look. His eyes glinted from within it's shadow'

'Yes, corp. We're over from Christmas Island', Robbie believed that stating the obvious always gave you the advantage; put the other person on the back foot. If they felt at all in charge they would have to tell you that they knew that and start again.

'We know that,' said the burly corporal, just been chatting to our HPD friend about you rushing over the road. Naughty boys.'

Sam and the others adopted a suitably contrite pose which seemed to please the policeman.

'Keep your noses clean,' he paused then a broad smile lit his face up, 'bastards these local police. Bastards with guns,' he laughed. 'Been over to Hickam yet?'

'No corp, we did arrive there but haven't been back.'

'Get over there for breakfast. It's the best thing you'll ever taste and it'll save you money. Fill you up for most of the day, free of charge. Nip over, you'll love it.' He smiled again and the two of them continued their slow walk up the street.

'Three fucking police forces!' Geordie cursed.

'Why did the Geordie cross the road?' Mickey Doyle piped up.

'I don't know, 'why did the Geordie cross the road?' Sam slipped into the music hall routine.

'To find out about a free breakfast. Fucking obvious,' said Mickey as they headed off in search of a massage parlour.

The first time.

Sam had already wondered about the business of getting some sexual gratification other than the five fingered widow which most men relied upon in the absence of female company. He had wondered aloud to Robbie how one might go about arranging this deal. Robbie had, as always, given a slick and probably correct answer but that still did nothing to further the scene that Sam had played in his head ever since the mention of massage parlours. It was the getting started in such a strange surrounding that was causing the problem.

When Sam had passed out from his training cadre aged eighteen and six months he had, as was the custom, been taken up to London on a coach with the rest of the lads for an evening out. This outing was to mark the end of training, the end of being ordered about just for the sake of being ordered about. From this point on you would be ordered about with a purpose.

He had been with his two mates; Smiffy and Lofty. These three had survived boys service and training camp, had come through, whilst not with honours, at least with something of their individual personalities intact. It had rained in London that evening and the pavements glittered with the lights from the Soho street signs. They had found a pub that sold beer at a reasonable price, steadied themselves with a drink and were now in search of... well, they didn't know. Excitement.

Smiffy was from deepest Norfolk where sex of the dirty kind was unknown. Lofty had a much more promising background having come into the army from a good family but had steadfastly insisted on being just a sapper rather than going on to become an officer which he could have become. Sex had rarely featured in his conversation. Sam, although a Londoner, had been too young to venture 'up town' by himself and so knew only those places that his Dad had known; offices, army buildings places that meant nothing to him. The umbrella blocking their path, wielded by a tall, fur coated woman, in effect stopped three country bumpkins.

'Five pounds, short time,' she had announced. Excitement had found them.

Two taxis had arrived and the tall girl allowed Lofty to open the door for her leaving the other taxi for Smiffy and Sam. The plump blonde one had gathered them into the cab sitting them on the fold down seats that faced the wide rear seat.

'Eileen,' she had introduced herself as she took the fiver and pressed it into her hand bag, 'and this is Joan.' Joan was likewise stowing Smiffy's fiver. The taxi had set off along the street turning into a broad road and gathering speed. Eileen pushed her hand between Sam's legs checking that the piece was in working order, which it was.

'Get it out then,' Sam obliged and for the first time in his life felt a woman roll a French letter onto his penis. She pushed herself forward in the seat and he entered her letting the fold up seat thump into place behind him.

He remembered the sensation now as he walked the warm Honolulu pavement. The light coming into the cab from the street, the two girls with their blouses open showing their tits, his eighteen year old libido on fire with lust as he pushed into her and then the final release. He had thrown his head back and caught sight of Buckingham palace lit up against the black sky. Eileen had held onto him tightly for a moment as the spasms subsided and then had gently disengaged and begun the tidying up process. The cab had turned into a narrow street and there they were. Getting out onto the pavement where they had been moments before. Short time, fiver each. The girls had said goodnight and Eileen had leaned toward him.

'Now you're a man love. Night.'

Lofty had appeared and the three new 'men' had started off along the pavement once more feeling... Sam never knew what he had felt but he never believed that it had been sordid and yet that was how most people would have describe it. Eileen had been gentle. Had she known it was his first time?

'D'you think anyone'll know we been shaggin' ' Smiffy

had asked as he led the way in front of Sam and Lofty, his braces still dangling from beneath his tunic.

'Silly sod,' Sam thought, 'wonder where he is now?'

Massage

The massage parlour looked sumptuous. Frighteningly sumptuous.

'Buggered if I'm going in there man!' Geordie looked across the road and held back.

'You'll be ok,' Robbie eyed the place, 'no cops, no walk signs.'

'You go then.'

Robbie hesitated, 'I was thinking I might get a drink along at that big hotel at the end there.

'Oh for fuck's sake,' Sam headed across the road and pushed through the glass doors. He looked round at his three friends still on the other side of the road and watching intently to see what he would do. He decided maybe it wasn't a good idea and turned toward the door.

'Good afternoon Sir, are you in need of relaxation because if you are I can tell you that you have come to the right place.' The speaker was the most beautiful woman Sam had ever seen. Her hair shone golden, her smile was broad and welcoming, her eyes as blue as a summer sky. Sam tried to speak, tried to tell her that it was not a good idea that he should come in and ask for sex and that the best thing he could do was to wish her a good day and head back across the road join the other three and find a bar.

'I would like a massage, please. Yes, that would be nice.' he heard himself say. There followed a question and answer with dozens of choices. Massages that defied Sam's limited knowledge of the subject. These choices were considerably reduced as the price list was discussed and he eventually chose the most basic treatment that was on offer. He was handed a white towelling robe and bath sheet, directed to a changing room, instructed to shower then proceed to the massage room. Like an automaton he followed the orders completely under the spell of the dazzling blonde.

    In twenty minutes he found himself back on the pavement feeling relaxed and scented and vaguely mystified by the whole process. He took the bus back to the YMCA and lay down on the bed in the cool, fusty room. The blonde had been something, he really meant something. She was the nearest thing that he had ever seen to what he imagined a film star would look like. Her figure, her lips, her eyelashes... his imagination flew over her body. He felt himself becoming erect and worked himself to a climax in the quiet room. As he relaxed so he looked back at the reality of the situation.

    His masseur had been a small, dark skinned Hawaiian who had introduced himself as Joe. This man had pushed and pummelled his muscles, oiled and rubbed them until Sam had finally relaxed and dismissed any discussion that might have led to some extraordinary activity. Joe had smiled his good bye and bade him return should he ever feel tense. At that price, Sam had decided, tenseness could be best seen off with a beer or two.

CHAPTER 10

More America

Hickam breakfast.
    Hickam field, the US air force base, had promised breakfast before nine any morning. Mickey and Sam had taken the bus. Sam leaving Robbie asleep, dead to the world after a long evening drinking, and Mickey doing the same for Geordie who had stirred just as he was leaving.

    'I'll bring you back a mug of tea,' he had said and Geordie had nodded his thank you from his dream world of Christmas Island and gone back to sleep.

    They made their way into the canteen.

    'Jeezus,' Mickey stood amazed. For a moment they both gazed as if they had entered a cathedral. This was a restaurant, not a military canteen, not a mess hall, not a cookhouse. It was light and airy, filled with airmen and women eating, talking. The air smelled of fresh coffee.

Sam felt totally bewildered. In an army cookhouse there was a long counter, same as school really. Here there were island counters laden with biscuit jars, packs of cereal, cold drinks, coffee pots. Looking for the familiar he headed toward the serving counter where trays of eggs, trays of bacon, trays of...? Certainly not fried bread...

'Hash browns man. Got yo I dee?' The speaker was a tall black man with a broad smile.

Sam produced his ID card. 'Royal army, hey.' the smile widened even more. 'Guess you's lost with all these goodies. Try this,' he pointed; 'from over there a flapjack with some maple syrup. Some orange juice to freshen the palette, then come up an' see me and have some bacon, scrambled eggs, hash browns with tomatoes and mushrooms. Coffee to follow and no need to eat 'til evenin'. Over there. Go' Sam went into his automaton mode and did as the negro had said. Everything smelled so good. Not just the food but the whole place. He helped himself to pancakes.

'First time for everything,' he told Mickey as the taste of maple syrup on salty pancakes filled his mouth. 'These guys certainly know how to eat.' He was beginning to speak like an American... 'these guys?' not surprising really, the whole culture was totally unlike the England that he had left behind; totally addictive.

'Did you go to the massage parlour?' he asked.

'Yeah.' Mickey mopped syrup from his plate. The vast busy canteen murmured behind them.

'What did you think?'

'OK' Mickey cleared his plate.

'Yeah, but did you get sex?'

'Did you?

Sam hesitated. He felt that he could urge no further information from Mickey without admitting his own failure. 'No,' he said.

'Me neither,' Mickey grinned, 'and I wasn't going to ask

Joe for a wank. What about the bird in reception though? I thought she was gonna turn up anytime, then Joe comes in and beats seven shades of shit out of me.'

'Did Robbie and Geordie go in?'

'No. Went off drinking down the road. That's when I figured that I would go in.' They both stood and headed for the serving counter.

Mickey turned to Sam, 'Looking at the price list, though, I reckon that even if sex had been on offer it would have been way beyond our pockets.'

Sam agreed and helped himself to a hash brown and some eggs. The negro smiled his sunshine smile. It made them both feel good with the day. Sam remembered something from his reading, something about a smile being like sunshine on wax: it softens. Plates heaped they headed for a table and began to eat.

'Hey, you guys royal army?' The speaker, a broad shouldered airman in uniform hauled a chair from the next table and straddled it. 'Gus Brandenburger' he reached out and shook their hands. Sam introduced himself and Mickey and confirmed that, yes, they were Royal Engineers.

'You have to excuse us Yanks,' Gus grinned, 'but Royal Navy, Royal Air Force then on down, Royal Signals; Royal Army just covers the lot. What I wanted to ask was are you coming over to the base for Friday night?'

'You're not serving an evening meal?' Mickey looked hopeful and Sam wondered where the little guy from Sunderland put all this food. Hollow legs, step mother would have said.

'Fourth of July. Sure there'll be snacks and drinks and a band and women, fireworks. We've had a few of you guys in this week and you're all invited.

'That's independence day?' Sam wondered.

'You got it. Don't worry, you'll be our guests. Get here around seven, it'll be a great evening. Bring your girlfriend if you have one.' He shook their hands again and left them. They ate in silence. Sam never ceased to be surprised by the Americans. His only experience was really from films. They were all cowboys or gangsters or soldiers fighting in a war. He reasoned that really you only made films about extreme characters. Ordinary people didn't get much of a look in when Hollywood did choosing. He imagined how boring a film would be about his own life. A life where really nothing exciting happened. Looking round him now he saw ordinary people. He spotted two girls not far away, talking earnestly as they ate, their hats pushed through their epaulettes, their hair pulled back and gathered in tight knots behind their heads. They looked so glamorous even in uniform. The blonde glanced his way and he realised he had been staring.

The breakfast proved the negro cook right. They headed back into town full to the brim and spent the rest of the morning wandering through the hotels and bars.

Technicolor was Sam's main impression of the place; all the buildings white or red with greens clashing in the bright sunshine. The police on their Harleys, the already glamorous bikes decorated with fringed leather saddles and chrome fittings. The cops themselves always in sunglasses that reflected your face when they spoke to you. The palms seemed greener here. On the island they looked bleached of colour, here they seemed the result of too much colour. The streets bustled. The people wore bright flowered shirts. The grey of England seemed more like an early film in Sam's imagination.

'What d'you reckon then?' Mickey broached the subject of the fourth of July dance at the air base.

'Yeah...' Sam was always wary of dances. You could get asked to dance.

Robbie and Geordie caught up with them and the idea was tossed around. Robbie eventually decided it would be well worth it but then made the proviso that they all share in a taxi to come back again as the busses would probably have stopped running by the time he'd had enough to drink.

'Moneys got to be watched,' he said, 'I don't mind sharing the cost but, you know, four musketeers and all that, one for all and all for one. Good idea?'

'We could always give blood,' Geordie said, out of the blue.

'Taxi drivers won't take blood,' Sam wondered if the

drink was perhaps having an effect on his friend.

'Twat! If you give a pint of blood you get five dollars. Bloke who came over a while back got back on the island white as a sheet but still had money in his pocket.'

'Bugger that,' Sam voiced the consensus, 'we all leave together.'

The Dance

'You were staring!' She said.

Sam turned to find a blonde fixing him with her wide blue eyes. For a moment he was nonplussed then her face registered as the girl he had seen at breakfast the morning before.

'I was. Sorry.' He felt himself reddening and thanked the lord for his island tan. Unable to think straight he said 'hi' and realised he was turning into an American.

'Hi. I'm Jo all the way from Beaufort, North Carolina and you must be...'

'Sam... all the way from Christmas Island, well London really it's just that I am...' he faltered realising that the blue eyes held his so intensely they made thought impossible.

'So you are Royal Army,' she turned to her friend who Sam now saw, once out of the blue eyed beam, was the girl who had been sat opposite Jo in the canteen. 'Sal, meet Sam of the Royal Army. Sam this is Sally.' The dark haired girl extended her hand and Sam felt very formal as he shook it.

Jo fixed him with her blue eyes once more. 'So tell me about London,' she said guiding him away from Sal who was talking to Mickey Doyle.

Tell her about London. He wouldn't know where to begin with this girl in front of him. She stood about his height, blue eyes, her hair now piled into a soft bun. Her smile broad, her teeth even and gleaming as only American teeth could. Say something, he told himself.

'Not much to tell and before you ask we don't get to meet the Queen every day.'

'Oh, that is so sad,' she said, her face taking on a look of mock disappointment, 'I guess you'll just have to dance with me to make up for it.' She took his hand and led him onto the dance floor. Sam remembered that he could not dance, well not this sober. Back in Trowbridge they had gone to the hop well oiled with Cuthbert Specials. Here he had only had a pint of Yankee beer which tasted a bit weak. Jo began to jive leaving Sam to work something out quickly. A look round the floor should have been reassuring; jiving for the most part but some just stood and swayed and others clung together probably to prevent a fall. As it was he just held her hand high and she whirled to the music. The band played a whole medley of rock songs and Sam swayed and held Jo's hand. Fortune kicked in and the music slowed. Jo came close and they began to sway. She was so light, he smelled her hair, felt her warmth pressed against him, soft.

The music ended and she led him to a seat.

'I'm sorry,' Sam began, 'never could dance sober.'

'You did fine,' she smiled her beautiful smile, 'never did tell me about London.'

'Big, old, grey, still got bomb sites from the war,' how could he explain such a drab place to this gleaming girl on this Technicolor island? 'getting better I suppose. What about Beaufort? Where is that?'

'North Carolina,' Sam raised his eyebrows. 'East coast, south of New York...? near Jacksonville?' Sam still looked puzzled, 'Don't they teach you guys anything. I live just back from the river which is really only a bit of sea behind an island. Then the Atlantic takes over. Lots of boats and sailing, nice weather most of the year, you'd love it.'

As she spoke Sam watched her eyes. They smiled, peeked, twinkled. Her eyes said all the unsaid things.

'Hey! Jo, where you been?' a tall American with a brutal crew cut towered over them, a glass in his hand, shouting over the band music.

'This guy bothering you?' He swayed and Sam realised the guy was really drunk. 'Don't worry,' Jo said to Sam, 'he thinks he's my boyfriend,' she stood up and pushed against his chest. The guy stumbled but then brushed her aside and came toward Sam. Leaning down he put the glass on the table and hauled him upright with ease.

Sam had never been a fighter. Dad had boxed but the idea of hitting people with fists had never caught on with his son. Always seemed to hurt his fists rather than the other way round. The one thing he did remember was that when a big guy has his hands full he may just use his knee or head to get the first blow home. Sam twisted his head presented an ear and caught sight of Geordie Thompson and Mickey Doyle coming towards him. Dangling like a rag doll he figured his options were limited but then Geordie pushed his way between them coming up amid the big American's arms, like some sort of party game. Facing Sam he pushed against his chest forcing the American's arms straighter and straighter. With a sudden release he brought his elbow back into the Yank's middle, grunting into Sam's face. The guy let go and crumpled to the ground. Geordie turned, almost as if dancing and held the big man by the shoulders as he collapsed to the floor choking.

'I think he swallowed something,' he called out to a group nearby. They ran across and knelt beside the coughing American.

'Hey Jimmy, what you swallowed eh? don't try to talk, hey, someone, get some water here.' He began to thump the American on the back causing him to choke more. 'Breath deep, Jimmy. Don't try to talk.' The glass of water appeared.

'Come on mate,' Geordie took Sam by the hand and steered him gently to the exit. Mickey found Robbie. 'Time to go, man. Just walk slow.'

Jo stood to one side, her eyes sad. She mouthed the word 'sorry' and Sam hesitated. Geordie hustled him on. 'No man.'

They headed out of the base and picked up a taxi back into town. Later, over a quiet drink in the Scotsman's bar, they talked it over.'

'Bloody women, mate. Trouble, trouble, trouble, stick to the booze.' Geordie grinned, 'She was a cracker though.'

'I could find her again,' Sam said.

'No you fucking couldn't, I'm not having another crack at that big bastard. You stay well clear.'

'What'd you hit him with?'

'Elbow in the solar plexus.'

Sam remembered Dad's boxing defence against a punch there. Once hit you could scarcely breath let alone stand up. The abiding image would be the friend feeding the fallen Jimmy water and Jimmy spluttering like it was poison.

Reflection

'We never did get to see the fireworks,' Robbie lounged in one of the cane seats on the patio of the Ala Moana hotel and looked out over the beach squinting his eyes against the sunlight and his cigarette smoke.

'Sam had enough bloody fireworks of his own to contend with, eh mate?' Mickey Doyle patted Sam's shoulder and grinned, 'mind, that Jo was a sparkler,' he laughed at his own joke.

The mention of Jo caused Sam a pang. She had seemed so right. The one who would have shown him how to enjoy himself on this Technicolor island. What did he do all day? Mooch from cafe to bar to beach and then to cafe, bar and bed.

'We should explore,' he said, 'Have a look at Pearl harbour; there's a memorial or something.' Sam looked around the group. None of them seemed particularly interested and he wondered why he considered going to see a memorial to man's stupidity and cruelty should be considered a holiday activity. These guys ate drank and lounged about. That was the holiday from getting up and doing hard work under a constant sun all day. Maybe they were right. Do nothing. Drift in this empty paradise.

'What about Diamond Head?'

'It's an extinct volcano you know...' Robbie dragged on his cigarette and was about to air his knowledge of extinct volcanoes when Geordie butted in,

'OK, we go up there, what if it goes off?'

'It's extinct, twat.'

'OK, becomes unextinct. We'd be right in the shit then.'

'We'd be right in the shit sitting here if it went off,' Mickey Doyle grinned, 'I'd get a bus to Hickam and get on the first plane out!'

'Right, we go up the mountain over there and what?' Geordie raised his eyebrows waiting for an answer.

'Great view,' Sam wondered if he was winning them over. At least they were talking about it.

'Of the Pacific! I've had enough of the bloody Pacific to last me a life time. Your turn to get them in. He pushed his empty glass toward Sam.

'Hey, lets move inside, it's gonna rain.'

Sure enough the legendary three o'clock shower began. The locals said that's why it was a paradise, you knew that come three you had to be in having a coffee while the rain God refreshed the streets and settled the dust. Sam went to the bar and watched as Diamond Head faded to a gentle grey through the rain.

CHAPTER 11

Convent

Saint Joseph's

He remembered watching the rain from the convent window. The convent was before Montrose. He was John then. It was not until he went to school that he became Sam. Robinson had decided that Sam Smart tripped off the tongue better than John Smart. Sam he had become. But now, in the convent, he was still John Smart and his best mate was Pinky so called because of his pink striped pullover.

These two had watched the storm along with the other children from the back windows of Saint Joseph's convent in Burgess Hill, Sussex. They gazed at the long line of hills that had born the brunt of the storm, waiting to see if there would be anymore lightning.

'They're the Downs, the South Downs,' Pinky said, 'Sister Vincent told me.'

'They look bigger now,' John pointed, tracing the curve of the hills that did indeed look bigger.

'That's because of the lightning I 'spect.' Pinky was a bright little boy whose imagination created an explanation for everything. 'Been flashing through the ground and churned it all up. Made 'em higher.'

'What about the people on the other side,' said John, 'will they be able to climb over them?'

'What, the Crusaders?' Pinky regarded his friend quizzically.

'Are there Crusaders there?' John glanced anxiously at the hills.

Pinky smiled. 'Crusaders and Saracens, and beyond is Jerusalem, the city for which they fight. Sister Vincent told me, Jerusalem and martyrs beyond them hills.'

They fell silent as the sun came out lighting the dark cloud that had made them look so high. The hills were lower now. 'Easier to cross.' John thought anxiously.

Beyond the Downs Brighton's streets, fresh washed by the rain, gathered pace once more.

When Mum had died, just at the end of the war, Dad, still in the army had placed him in a children's home in Muswell Hill. He remembered seeing the tower of Alexandra Palace, something to do with the BBC. Mum's sister Jean was also still in the forces, a Wren and so he presumed they had been hard pushed to look after him in the circumstances. The home had been brief and Sam could remember little of it. Dad had moved him from there into the convent school; Saint Josephs, in Burgess Hill. A big house with gardens overlooked from a terrace. A paradise?

He remembered the room of his arrival, Dad gone to discuss business with the nuns. It was a cold room with pale green walls and a big bay window looking out onto some trees. He did not go near the window but instead lay down on one of the two empty beds, the only warmth his back against the blanket. From there he could see the blind sky beyond the window. The ceiling was high and he watched some flies that danced in the corner. They made no noise.

'Country flies,' he thought. Not like city flies; fat from spilled food. Bluebottles that buzzed against the inside of shop windows.

The door opened and a nun peeked in at him, her pale face framed in white cotton beneath a black bombazine veil. He got off the bed and stood up.

'That's all right,' she had said, speaking softly 'lay you back down. Here...' she reached among the folds of her habit and brought out a small slip of paper. 'Irish sweepstake ticket...' She held it for him to see, 'Horses. You have it.' She gave him the slip, 'now lay you back down but take those sandals off before you do. I shall come and collect you for tea soon' And so she left him, her habit seeming to contract through the doorway, flouncing and black, making her look like a bat finding a niche.

He took his sandals off and lay back on the bed turning the ticket over in his hand. Two horses vied to pass a golden winning post. He turned it over. The back was green and filled with tiny print. He held the ticket close to his chest and closed his eyes. He was seven and he had a coloured ticket to play with.

Convent routine.

Convent life was structured. Roman Catholic and structured. He had been taken down to tea and had knelt on the hard, black brown wooden form while grace was said. He would try to sit on the window side of the table as this meant that he knelt with his tummy to the table. Sit on the other side and you had to kneel with your bottom against the table and the ever present threat of falling forward onto the floor! Unable to step he would have landed face down.

Melted cheese - he knew no other name for it - became his favourite dish. Making dough balls of bread his first skill and Pinkie became his first friend. Pinkie because he wore a pink pullover. Pinkie who knew the ins and outs and had helped him avoid the pitfalls that could raise the wroth of Sister Vincent.

The barman slid the tray of drinks toward him and he fished the dollars from his wallet. They were getting less he thought as he carried the tray over to the lads. The rain was easing, Diamond head becoming more defined.

Sister Vincent had a hard chiselled, plain face that meant business. The rope about her waist hung in a long end with three knots tied at intervals. Sam regarded the rope as a threat. It looked the sort of rope that could scourge naughty children, the sort of rope that one associated with martyrs. Martyrs featured heavily in Sam's education during the convent period. Martyrs and potatoes.

The days started with Mass. John became chosen to be a left hand altar boy. This was the start of the promotional ladder that would lead to him becoming a right hand altar boy. Beyond that he did not know. He wore a black cassock and a white, starched surplice.

The priest, Father Auvey, would dress in sumptuous robes; gold and green with a satin shine. He and the two altar boys would process to the chapel, marching silently across the diagonal of the empty, wood floored, wood panelled, hall. The routine was never changing and John progressed to right hand altar boy and would hold the water jug while the priest washed the sacred host crumbs from his fingers. The smallest drop of water. The fingertips gently cleansed. He was fascinated by the pure delicacy of the whole thing. The censer and its incense, the little cluster of brass bells, the lighting and snuffing of the six candles behind the altar, the monstrance with the host behind its little glass fronted circle, the brass rays spreading and catching the coloured light from the windows. The entire thing was wonderful.

After Mass came breakfast and then potatoes.

The Angelus

The cellar was downstairs which sounds obvious. John knew that cellars were downstairs. The thing that surprised him was that when he went downstairs the cellar opened out onto the garden and so the sunshine would beam into the whitewashed arched vault. They would sort the potatoes, rubbing the dried earth from them, their hands pink against the rough brown tubas. The Angelus bell would ring...

'Hail Mary full of grace, blessed be thy name...' they would chant kneeling on the stone floor, then pick the next potato up, bead two of their improvised rosary. John wondered if the potatoes had been blessed. An unblessed rosary was no good. Sister Vincent had told them. A rotten potato had squashed and oozed black slime over his hands, the smell made him retch and he had been marched to the scullery to wash in the big stone sink. He stood on the box and adjusted the tap flow to a glasslike stem of cold water then he had washed the slime from his fingertips with the same small movements that Father Auvey used. The slap across his bare legs stung

'Wash the Devil's putrescence from your hands and stop fiddling about.' Sister Vincent. Ever present.

CHAPTER 12

Loretta

The Hula lesson

Hula lessons were worth watching. All sorts, mainly female but occasionally some rotund older men, would gather in the large foyer of the Ala Moana hotel and be coached through the subtleties of the native dance. Sam enjoyed watching and had to admit to himself that perhaps he was a little envious of these extrovert people who seemed wholly unconcerned that they were perhaps making a fool of themselves.

'Silly sods.' Geordie passed his northern judgement and drifted off to the games room. He and Robbie had become dab hands at a sort of billiards. No balls just flat pucks that skidded over the glass plate of the table. Sam remembered playing the same sort of game with pennies and a comb in the science room at school. He preferred the hula classes. The arm movements, as if pushing a lover away and then the come hither of the finger tips. Why did fingertips fascinate him so?

A fat man in glasses, a straw pork pie hat perched high on his balding head, wiggled as instructed. The pretend grass skirt rode lower on his hips as he moved and his come hither hands took a break every now and then to hitch it back up with each pass of the music.

'He'll lose it in a minute.' A girl at the next table smiled and nodded toward the unlikely dancer.

'Hope his shorts stay up then,' Sam turned toward her on the long wall seat. She smiled and looked back to the swaying dance group. She was slim with a sharp profile, straight nose, firm chin, her golden hair cut to her jaw. A shoulder bag and sunglasses lay on the table in front of her. How long had she been there? Sam knew that he would have seen her; his time on the island had made him seek out women as if his life depended on it and yet here was this girl not two feet away with an empty glass in front of her. She must have been there ages.

'Would you like another drink?' he ventured. 'Mickey and I are both dying of thirst.' he picked up Mickey Doyle's glass ready to make for the bar.

'No,' she said, 'I'm fine.'

'Nonsense, you're empty,'

'Ok,' she nodded, her hair gentling against her face, and slid the glass toward him. 'Just a coke; too early for alcohol.'

When he returned with the tray of drinks she had moved into his seat and was in deep conversation with Mickey.

'This lass is from Washington.'

'Great,' said Sam wondering how he had missed the trick.

'Washington DC' continued Mickey, 'not Washington County Durham.'

'Maybe the accent gives it away,' she said and Sam became aware of her accent being light and almost clipped, not the drawl that he usually associated with Americans.

'D'you think they named the DC one after the County Durham one, typing error maybe?' Sam asked, placing the drink in front of her and sitting where she had sat.

'Not likely man. The one in County Durham is just a

little village. Come again written on the back of the welcome sign! River runs through twice a week. Tiny. Anyway it'd be the wrong way round, Durham County! Hey that sounds yankee to me.' They all laughed.

    She now sat between them dividing her attention as the conversation continued it's unimportant way. Sam wondered how he could engage her once more. Mickey was wittering on like a train, his Sunderland accent apparently mesmerising the girl.

    'Sam Smart,' he introduced himself, 'and this is Mickey Doyle from the North of England, a different race altogether.'

    'Loretta,' she took his hand, 'Leicher, from Washington District Columbia, if'n you want the full title. You're from England too?'

    'London.' Sam was always pleased to say the capital was his home. At least most people had heard of it. At home he would add Chelsea as his birth place to further egg the pudding. The fact that it was Saint Stephan's hospital which catered for a large proportion of London births was not explored unless he wanted to talk himself down in the face of aggression.

    The Hula instructor came across and confronted the three of them. A big native woman she looked as if she would be difficult to cross.

    'We need some extra folk for this lesson an' you three look just the right three to me.' She grinned her broad Hawaiian smile. Mickey rose but excused himself muttering about a call of nature that had to be urgently answered. Sam protested that he could not dance, an argument that proved futile.

    'That's why we gonna teach you, then you will be able to dance; lucky, lucky lucky'.

    Sam shrugged and Loretta smiled. 'Come on, it'll be fun, she said and they joined the group and were shushed into line ready for the lesson. The fat American stood next to Sam. He leaned over. 'When you get yer grass skirt pretend it's a bit loose and that girl on the end there will adjust it for you,' he explained mysteriously, 'put your arms up and keep your eyes down, oh boy! best pair of tits on the island.' He winked and sure enough a young Hawaiian girl came and girded the pretend grass skirt about his waist. Sam looked down, then toward Loretta.

'Maybe I should take these jeans off,' he raised his eyebrows and smiled.

'Don't you dare!' she giggled and swung her own skirt, the plastic fronds swishing over her shorts.

The Hula girls began their lesson, speaking of Chants and Songs. Hands were positioned, movements demonstrated, steps learned. The music began and Sam lived again that awful moment of realisation that comes from trying to dance when you know you can't. Making it worse he spotted his three friends seated along the seat opposite ready to clap their support but already doubled with laughter.

When they got to the end of the dance, all laughing and the onlookers applauding, they went to the little table paid a dollar and got a certificate with their names written in and signed by the Kumu Hula which they figured was the instructor.

'I can put this up in class when I get back home.' Loretta settled the slip into her bag.

'Class?' Sam queried.

'Sure. I teach school.'

'Do school teachers go to the pictures?'

She stopped walking and turned toward him looking puzzled.

'Films, you know'

'Oh! movies! Sure they do.

'Would you like to go to the pictures with me?' he risked the question quickly before they got back to the table where his three mates sat, grinning like Cheshire cats.

'When?'

'This evening?'

'Yeah, I guess. What's showing?' her eyes held his as if the decision was still in the balance.

'I don't know but we can find out. Where are you staying?'

'Here. The Ala Moana. Hold tight a moment.' She strode off to the desk and quizzed the clerk. Sam waited.

'Ok. The Vikings? Sound good? Cinema in South King Street. Pick me up here about six thirty?'

Sam nodded, a bit dazed at the turn of his luck. They walked back and joined the others. As they approached she took his arm and squeezed it. 'Hey! we're hula dancers don't you feel good?' and she bumped her hip against his.

Sam felt magically good.

The Pictures

To certain people there are things in life that are so good they are frightening. 'Frightfully good!' the upper crust say. 'Frighteningly good', thought Sam as he prepared for his evening date. Suddenly he was scared. What was a lovely school teacher doing going to the pictures with a thick squaddie from Tooting. He had to go, wanted to go but was frightened. Would he mess it up?

'Nervous?' Robbie watched his preparations.

'Nah. Yeah. I don't know. What if I mess it up?'

'Concentrate on getting her into bed is my advice.' Robbie looked at his watch, 'You've got five days mate. Take it easy, nothing to lose.'

'Robbie was right,' he thought, 'nothing to lose, just be yourself.' He didn't think that he stood much chance of getting into bed with her; too classy. Still nothing to lose.

'Did you enjoy it?' she asked as they came out of the pictures into the cool Hawaiian evening and began to walk slowly back to her hotel. The nearest he had ever been to paradise. He wanted so much to kiss her, to complete the idyll.

'Yes,' Sam wondered what else to say. He had spent the majority of the time in the cinema wondering if he should put his arm around her shoulders. The very thought of finding an excuse to lift his arm – scratch his nose maybe? – seemed so corny. In the end he had not. The mental struggle had interfered with his understanding of the plot.

'There was a lot of back slapping,' he said finally.

'That was to reinforce their toughness.' She turned and smiled at him, then threaded her arm through his. 'You come from England, did you get taught about the Vikings?'

'If I did I missed it.' He suddenly felt incredibly thick. He had no idea whether the Vikings had 'rabbed and plundered' as Kirk Douglas had put it in his no nonsense American accent, 'you're a teacher, you should know.'
'I think the eight sixties marked one set of Viking battles.' she smiled and stopped walking, then placed her hand on her forehead, 'I may be wrong but the King in the movie, Aelle got killed along with King Osbert,' She turned and took his arm once more.
'So he didn't get fed to the wolves then?'
'No. I think that was a bit of movie horror, designed to pull the audiences in. Directly the spy told Ernest Borgnine about the wolf pit you knew it just had to come in sometime. Come on, it's time for a nightcap, my treat. Enough blood and thunder for one night. Smell the jasmine.' She tilted her head back. 'We should have a nightcap.'
'Not cocoa?'
'No, something exotic from the bar.'
Sam followed meekly, totally captivated by this slight girl, overcome with the beauty of the place, it was everything home wasn't: lights everywhere, warm balmy air, the smell of jasmine and this lovely girl. He felt himself sliding into... what? Love. He had only known her five minutes but already he knew she was different. Someone special.
He had pecked at her cheek when they said goodnight. They agreed another date. Sam walked back to the YMCA in a dream.

'Get your end away then?' Robbie sat up in bed bleary eyed from drink and tiredness.
'Not yet,' He climbed into bed and remembered the soft pale cheek and her perfume mingled with jasmine.

Diamond head

'So why did you become a teacher?'
They were on Diamond head in the vast park that had been created on the dead volcano. It was their second date. She had taken the reins and insisted that they go up and admire the

view. 'Start at the top and work down,' she had twinkled naughtily at him.

'Teaching. Second choice,' she sipped her drink and Sam watched the honey gold of her hair brushing her pale cheek. She wore a floppy straw hat with a yellow flower sewn into the band. 'Not smart enough to be a doctor,' she smiled. Sam wondered if he had touched a nerve.

'I'm sorry...'

'No. It's ok. Dad was a doctor. I guess I couldn't see further 'n' being that. It was sorta what you did; went to school then to U and got your medics degree then became a doctor - joined the family business, easy. At the end of high school one of my teachers pointed out that a love of English wouldn't be much use to a medico and my grades were a bit low so I followed his advice, went back to school and learned how to teach.'

'Do you like it?'

'Do you like being a soldier?' She watched him over the rim of her glass her eyes blue in the shade of her hat brim.

He looked out over the sea.

'Well, no, not really.'

'Then why be one? Do something else.'

'I signed on. I've got another seven, eight years to do yet. Costs money to buy yourself out.'

She held his gaze. 'You had to join, yeah?'

'Yeah, Dad insisted. I used to play truant...'

'Hooky!?'

'If that's not going to school, yep!'

'What'd you do when you played tru - ant?' She copied his accent for the word

'Nothing really. Went up London with a mate and looked at things; we didn't have any money so we just wandered about.'

'What did you see?'

'Nothing really, buildings, the river. Saw a man balancing a tennis racquet once, finishing it off before putting it in the box and selling it. We used to go in the museums; there's loads of them round Kensington.'

'And you saw nothing? Nothing but a guy finishing a

tennis bat? Come on!'

Sam suddenly saw the aimlessness that had marked his schoolboy self. He had wandered about in one of the world's finest cities, wandered into museums and then, quite seriously, had admitted to this slight girl that he had seen nothing. He felt ashamed of the admission. He attempted to excuse himself.

'We didn't know what to look for,' he said lamely.

'That's where you needed a teacher. You should have done your lookin' with me!'

Sam smiled remembering his companion on their truant outings.

'You'd 've loved Doc Shaw. Best mate, introduced me to 'tru ent', hooky!'

'Doc?'

'Derek Raymond Shaw. Dr Shaw. Crew cut blond hair. Loved sugar sandwiches.

Loretta pulled a face.

'Oh yeah, not too much of anything around in Britain during the early fifties so sugar sandwiches or condensed milk with cocoa powder. Not like you Yanks with loads of steaks and hot dogs...'

'Oooo! that's why I'm so fat,' she placed her hands on her slim waist, 'hundred and twenty, thirty at the most.'

'Stones!?'

'Pounds fool! Come on, let's walk and yes, I love teaching.'

The sea glittered all around the jut of the headland. The sun shone and Sam reached down and held her hand. He felt... He didn't know how he felt. This was too good to be true, there had to be a snag, some unforeseen drawback. He found it. Three days time he would have to fly back to Christmas Island. Back to heat, hard work, the smell of diesel and dust and no Loretta. Fact. The hot updraft threatened her hat and she let go his hand to save it.

The fact that he had bunked off school and yet done nothing with the free time that resulted whirled in his head as they walked off to find lunch. He had seen things, interesting things but it was as if he had taken the images and stored them away in a cellar rather than hanging them on the wall to be looked at, examined on a regular basis. He must start trying to make sense of the stored memories. They turned down the path toward a cafeteria and he took her hand again. Her small fingers felt fragile in his grip and he held them gently.

They ate ham with peaches and pineapple.
'What a combination.'
'Comes from the settlers,' she told him. 'Goin' west in a covered wagon you didn't have space to pack lots of crockery so, one tin plate, hunting knife and a fork. That's why we Yanks eat the way we do.'
'Is there anything you don't know?'
'Like I said, all the stuff I needed to be a doctor... and,' she held his gaze again, 'what makes Sam tick. I don't know that. Something must have got to you in life, something that lit up the world just a little brighter.' She took a cigarette from her bag and held it to her lips. Sam waited then realised she was waiting for it to be lit. He fumbled his lighter alight. 'Is that American?'
'What?'
'Waiting for a light.'
'Oh yes. A lady never lights her own cigarette if a gentleman is present.'
'What if he hasn't got a light, doesn't smoke?'
'Who doesn't smoke? C'mon. Don't dodge the question. Anything stick in your mind?'
'I did a reading competition once. Got picked out from our group to read two speeches on stage.'
'Tell me.' She leaned forward her elbow on the table her chin on the back of her hand.

CHAPTER 13

Realisation

The reading

When you entered the army as a boy soldier you were still entitled to free school milk. The incongruous sight of young men in first world war uniforms queuing at ten in the morning for a small bottle of milk and a slice of Madeira cake always amused Sam. Education didn't. He was back at school.

'You shouldn't worry about being in the classroom,' Tom Fullick had joined the same day as Sam, a country boy from Cheriton - 'wherever that was', thought Sam,

'Near Alresford,' Tom had said - 'wherever that was', thought Sam once more.

'You shouldn't worry about being in the classroom, if you aren't in there then they'll have you on the assault course or marching up and down or having your kit inspected. Much worse.'

Tom was round, not fat but solid made out of big pieces of meat and tanned like mahogany. Sam imagined him working in the fields and sure enough one evening he had entertained them all to a full version of 'To be a Farmer's Boy.' He liked Tom.

The class room had a stove when the weather got cold. Better than the windswept square. Their teacher was Warrant officer class one Jim Parkinson of the education corps. A round, white haired man with a round rosy cheeked face he would have them think about English.

'I want you to think now,' he said one afternoon, 'I want you to think about description. I want you to think about describing a light bulb to an African native who had never seen a light bulb. Are you thinking?'

Sam thought but could only think that surely they had light bulbs in Africa? He had seen films set in Africa and they always had light bulbs strung up in the warm night with moths flying into them. Take the native to see a Tarzan film and point them out when they came on. He put his hand up and told Mr Parkinson of his idea.

'You are a lazy boy,' came the puzzling reply. 'Lazy because you would let a film maker do your describing. Use what little imagination you have to communicate what you see when you look at a light bulb. What do you see?'

'A pear, Sir,'

'A pair of what?'

'No Sir, a pear from a pear tree. A pear made of ice, clear ice with the pips inside. You can see them through the ice.'

Mr Parkinson beamed. 'Where did that come from?.'

'Dunno, Sir. I just saw a pear only it was made of ice or glass. Perhaps the ice would melt in Africa.'

Parkinson kept him in after class and had him meet Miss Cox the WVS lady who looked after the library.

'Can you read?' she asked.

'Yes ma'am.'

'That started it' said Sam lighting another cigarette for them both. The breeze blew into the cafeteria and the three o'clock rain wet the road outside.

'I liked the description, did you really make it up?'

'Yep. No idea how but I did.'

'You said started it, started what.'

'Well Parky taught me to read, really read. When he asked me to see the light bulb he sort of pointed me in the right direction, held my head, made me look.' Miss Cox had me sorting second hand books that came in from lord knows where. I had to figure what they were, western, detective, that sort of thing. I came across a book on etiquette one day and couldn't figure how to pronounce it or what the subject was. She took time to tell me about it, had me read sections out loud. Parky would come in and help with the speeches he had chosen for me to read. Told me how they worked, what the speakers where trying to say.'

'What were the speeches?'

'Two Shakespeare: Quality of Mercy and Neither a borrower or a lender be. Two American; Gettysburg Address and the opening of the Declaration of Independence. I had to do two and chose Gettysburg and Quality of Mercy.'

'And ?'

'I won. Fell up the steps onto the stage for the first one which was the quality of mercy. Parky reckoned afterwards that the speech was right for the occasion. I needed all the mercy I could get. Gettysburg went without a hitch. Got a certificate somewhere.'

'Wait a minute,' she hauled her chair closer to the table and set both elbows firmly on it. 'you're telling me that you studied these two speeches, well four speeches, then delivered two of them. Studied them deep enough to understand them, deep enough to begin to feel the power of language yeh and then you won the competition...'

'It was only a little competition...'

'Doesn't matter a damn how big it was. You won it. Sam Smart the guy who 'went up London' and saw nothing 'cept a man finishing a tennis bat! This Mr Parkinson certainly found you. What have you done with his gift to you?'

'Done? I won the competition...'

'And then?'

'Well... I don't know, nothing really. I got swallowed up by the army. Army rules, army customs, army mates. There wasn't any way out.'

'Do you still read?'

'Not much.'

'You must read. If you can understand what you are reading - apply the lessons that Mr Parkinson showed you - then you can learn everything. Be like a sponge; soak it all up, remember it. You should keep a diary. Write down your thoughts.' She stopped and smiled. 'Sorry, teacher coming out. I just thought, you could be Smart by name and nature. Sound good?'

Sam nodded. 'It's stopped raining,' he said.

The Force field.

'You shagged her yet?' Geordie Thompson lit another cigarette pushing his empty plate away.

'Give it time,' Sam sipped his drink. He was playing for time. This girl was like no other girl he had ever known. To say he was frightened of her was not quite right, to say he respected her would have been nearer the truth but that emotion was new to Sam, not the word he would have used. It was as if he had come up against an invisible barrier, like the force fields the science fiction pictures were so fond of. It didn't hurt, not like a brick wall but he didn't know how to get beyond it. How to get to the point where they would make love - he hated the term shagged, something rough about it, something that suggested dominance rather than immersion and release, like doing a full crawl in the bath!

This girl baffled him. She came out with thoughts that scrambled his thinking.

'Have you ever wondered why light is invisible?' She asked. They were wandering on the beach she wearing the sun hat so as not to get her nose burnt.

'It isn't, Sam said, 'I can see it all around.

'Ah!,' she turned and twinkled at him, 'no you can't, you can only see the things it illuminates.' She held her fingers up, 'if you could see the light between them then you wouldn't be able to see my face.' She leaned into him, still with her fingers up on each side of her face then kissed him quickly on the nose.

He held her shoulders. 'It's a lovely face,' he said and kissed her gently on the lips.

His first real kiss since he had kissed Christine that cold night in Trowbridge. Now he kissed a beautiful girl on a warm beach in Hawaii. Sun all around. So different to that last hungry, lust fuelled, glutton's kiss with Christine; this kiss light, gentle.

Her hands strayed from the light lesson and cupped his face. Her body softened against him.

'That was nice,' she whispered. Sam felt his need of her beginning to take hold.

'Forbidden fruit, for both of us. Let's not go too far down this path.'

'Why? we're both grown up.'

'That's why we behave properly, because we are grown up. Think of it in a day or so you are going to fly back to your desert island and I am going to fly back to Washington. You will still be in the army for a few more years, in other countries meeting other girls. I will be in Washington teaching kids how to read. You can't afford to get out of the army and I want to teach kids in Washington. I want to teach them and think of my British soldier maybe thinking of me somewhere.'

'But you make it sound as if I am going to get you pregnant. I won't get you pregnant,' Sam felt the shallowness of the words as he spoke them.

'Famous first words. 'I didn't think you'd get pregnant' are the famous last words.' She pulled back from him. 'Lets enjoy this. What we have now, it will only last two more days and then be a memory. Let's enjoy this.'

Sam felt a great sob of sorrow, almost as if he was going to cry. He couldn't understand his feeling. He wanted to make love to her, enact the fantasies that had filled his mind as he lay in bed. And yet he knew that what she said was right. He had heard enough stories about guys having to get married. That was bad enough but what if the girl was in America and he was God knows where? Some might have thought 'perfect', no way of getting involved. He couldn't do that.

He pulled her to him. 'I know, you are right, it would be stupid. I'm sorry.'

She kissed him again. 'Don't you dare say you love me or I shall kick your shins.'

'OK, I won't say "I love you".' He stared hard at her as he said it and they both laughed.

Saturday

Saturday morning saw Sam still in bed at nine o'clock. Robbie lay sleeping in the next bed his hangover not yet active. Sam lay with a deep sense of misery spilling over from his troubled night. Saturday! Sunday would be their last day and he would have to say goodbye to Loretta. They would not meet until this evening; she had gone on a prearranged plane trip to fly over the other islands. Sam realised that as this was the point of her holiday, rather than an aimless British squaddie, it would have been silly for her not to go. Since meeting on Wednesday they had seen each other every day. She had made very clear the bounds of their relationship and such was her strength of character he had accepted that he could kiss her, hold her close and press her to him but there it stopped. No longer a glass force field but somehow a contract, an agreement that Sam was surprised to find comforting. He wondered briefly if this was how you found your wife!

His experience with girls had been to start with the sex. That, mostly, was as far as it got. This girl was different. She sparkled, she dazzled him.

He could not understand her beauty; Mickey Doyle had remarked that she was not a 'glamour puss' and yet her sparkle dazzled him.

Most of all they talked. Non stop it seemed. She quizzed him, about being a child in the war, about being in the army. She lamented his attitude to school but did explain that the broken nature of his childhood had meant that no one had explained school to him, meant that when other kids got the hang of learning in a particular school with a particular set of teachers he had moved on to a new situation, to a new set of teachers, rules and subjects that would be taught in a slightly different way. Like changing a maze halfway through when you were just beginning to get the hang of it. Somehow she made a lot of things clear; found the mystery then unravelled it for him. No one had ever done that before. He sighed. Now the person who did would soon be nothing but a memory.

Saturday. How would he get through to seven that evening? He decided he would buy her a present.

He got up and showered . Robbie stirred then sat up on the edge of the bed watching as Sam dressed.

'Heavy evening?' Sam asked.

'I think so, can't remember. Geordie got into a scrap with some big bloke so I left. Can't remember much after that. You off out?'

'Yep.'

'Meeting the love of your life again?'

'Not till tonight, I need to think. Tomorrow's our last day.'

'You sad about that?'

'Fucking right I am!' Sam's anger at the situation flashed. 'Yes, really pissed off.'

Robbie rubbed his head, mussing his normally neat hair. 'Don't do anything stupid, will you?'

'Like what?'

'I dunno. Just put it down to experience, we move on. Next week we'll be digging holes or building huts. You'll have forgotten her by then. Distant memory.'

'Yeah... I'm off.'

Robbie cradled his aching head. 'Jesus.'

Shopping

The strange notion entered Sam's head that the street in front of him was filled with butterflies. Thousands of brightly coloured wings seemed to beat the air mixing noise with light. His thoughts tumbled about the question; what should he buy for this girl?

'How silly,' he thought, 'I didn't know this girl last week and now she fills my entire world.' Maybe that was it, maybe he was a twat. He certainly wouldn't get his end away so that marked it down as a failure. A failure in this crowded street? Looking for something to please her in a world of colour and movement that shone in her invisible light.

Shopping in Hawaii is expensive, even if you know what you want.

Trinkets would be the thing and yet that sounded cheap even as he said it to himself and the trinkets were anything but cheap. The prices were crazy. A pair of shoes cost the same as a suit in Blighty and a suit cost the same as a pair of shoes back home. Maybe the Americans charged the Hawaiians a lot for leather.

'The yanks must have tons of the stuff,' he thought, remembering the vast stampeding herds in the cowboy films.

'When is a trinket not a trinket? A bangle is a trinket, a ring? Way out of range and too serious anyhow. A rosary? Was she a Catholic? Did they have Catholics in America?' The fact that he had heard of Gospel Music was as far as his knowledge of American spirituality went.

'Anyway,' he thought, 'that would be far too holy. Almost as bad as a ring.' Pictures of her in white with a ring on her finger and a rosary entwined about her hand made him stop. He turned into a coffee bar, one where they had been before, the one with the waitress who thought they serviced the Queen's Rolls Royce. She was there with the glass of water ready to take his order.

'You all by yo'self today?' she smiled producing the pencil from her piled hair and flipping the pad from nowhere again.

'That's right,' he said.

'You look like you found a girl, you waitin' fo her?'

'Sort of. She's on a trip today. I won't see her 'til this evening.'

'I get your coffee, that'll make the time go by.'

When she returned Sam told her the situation.

'How long you knowed this girl?'

'Four days to now. We have to say goodbye on Sunday, I fly back to Christmas bloody island then.' he paused on the edge of that thought. He felt the nearest he had ever felt to crying since he was a kid. Felt he could put his head in his hands and sob.

'Hey, she sure got you. Must be special, real special. No way you can meet up again?'

'No. Too much distance, too much army. She wants to carry on being a teacher and I have to carry on being a soldier for a few more years yet. Can't buy myself out and too scared to go on the run. No chance. I want to buy her a present but this place is so expensive and I'm down to my last few dollars. I'm stuck.'

'You don't need money honey, you need imagination. You have to give her something that she will always remember you by.'

'Too late for a photograph...'

'Na. Photo's fade, get lost, stuck in books that end up somewhere else. Na. Something that she can touch, something that will be a sign of your time together. Don't have to be expensive, does have to be lastin', a token of your few days in each other's arms. Oh my!' she fanned herself, 'gettin' all romantic me. I'll be crying in my coffee 'for I know it. Good luck. Remember, imagination, not money.' She hurried off to serve another customer leaving Sam staring out of the window and asking himself 'what lasts?'

Dad shopping

Tooting market provided a shortcut from Totterdown road to the high street. Well Dad said it did but Mum pointed out that it was only the other two sides of the same square. Through the market turn right into the High street. Not through the market, turn left and come to the other end of the market. Dad had nudged him, 'She's right but...' and here he grinned and guided his son to the stall of Cheap Jack. 'Piled high with everything and all of it cheap'. The pair of them rummaged through the bargains. Apple corers, rejected and Dad spotted rust on the tin blade. A thing for beating eggs. They had both watched the demonstration of this a week before. Watched the egg being broken and separated with the white being put into the tall plastic flask and the flat disc of the beater being pumped up and down so that the white fluffed into a solid looking mass. The demonstrator, a round man in a dark suit then added the yoke and poured the mixture into a small pan that sat over a little primus stove. The omelette cooked in no time at all and the man sliced it from the pan giving out portions on paper plates. The crowd loved it and bought the flask and beater it seemed by the dozen. Dad had bought one. The surprise came when the demonstrator rapped his knuckles on the pan getting the attention of the crowd while the boy still sold the beaters.

'Ladies and gentlemen,' he cried, 'you may not like my cooking but you'll love my washing up!' He gave a single wipe with a cloth and showed the pan clean with no egg clinging as was normally the case with Dad's cooking. 'Non stick!' he pulled a box from beneath the table and proceeded to sell the pans. Dad was impressed but fell short of buying one.

'Films!' Dad had spotted a box of Kodak roll film and bought four. 'Plenty of holiday snaps with this lot, twelve to a roll.' The pictures had been taken but some of the films were fogged. Sam thought it matched the weather that they usually had on their Scottish holidays. He wondered where the pictures were now. Probably with Grace. Did a step mother get to keep everything? Where the hell was his past? Real mum dead, Dad now dead. Grace was kind enough but he found her forbidding; in what way he could not say. He just felt not at ease in her presence. Why didn't he come from a family that started as one and stayed the course 'till the end. In one place, with people you knew around you, school mates that grew up with you. At each point the chopper had fallen and he had started anew in a strange place.

If only Cheap Jack's had been round the corner of this Hawaiian street.

The problem

The problem was how would he give this girl something to remember of him and Hawaii when he knew so little of Hawaii himself? He had drifted through the place - well until he had met Loretta - without really seeing it. Skimmed over what should have been a rich experience. She was off on a flight around the island, he could have done that. Well perhaps not, given the lack of dollars. She it was who dragged him up to Diamond Head, she it was urged him to question things. He didn't know anything compared with her. Dumbo Sapper Sam Smart.

His pessimistic self imposed on his thinking. Would she meet someone else on this flight? Some rich American guy with good looks and a ready smile. Wouldn't be much point in meeting soldier Sam again with some guy able to pay for a table at a posh restaurant. Jealousy flared making him angry. Why pay good money for a present when he would be gone on Monday and she could be with her new handsome American friend? He stopped still on the pavement.

'Get a fucking grip!'

Robbie hove into view.

'You still moping about. Look like a lovelorn tortoise.'

'What's that look like then?'

'You, you twat.'

'The trouble is that I really don't know anything about this place and I want to give her a present that will remind her of me.'

'A swift one mate. That'll remind her,' he grinned.

'Is that all you think about?'

'If I can help it, fancy a beer?'

They set off then Sam caught sight of the tourist office.

'That's the place.'

Robbie looked puzzled but followed him across the road.

The office seemed to be made of glass once more, the doors opened automatically for him as he had now grown to expect and sure enough once inside a dusky beauty of a girl approached with an offer of help. Robbie cheered up but Sam beat him to it.

'Hi. A friend of mine has gone on a plane trip around the islands, I wondered if you would know what route she would be taking?'

'Do you know where she went from, take off time?'

'Here, I suppose, main airport perhaps. This morning, she said it was early?'

'Probably not the main airport,' she smiled, 'most of these trips take off from private strips, don't worry, I'll make a call.' She swung behind the desk and phoned.

They were so organised. I'll make a call would be the last thing that could happen in England. Enquiries, yes. That meant they would ask someone else who didn't know. Pathetic.

'You're in luck. Only one set off early this morning. Island Bird. I'll show you.' She led the way between the stands to a huge map of the islands. It was criss crossed with lines showing all the tours on offer. She ran her finger down the index.

'Here you go, Island Bird is the blue line, see.' she turned away to be engaged in conversation by the ever eager Robbie.

Sam had not seen the map before and was surprised to see the group of islands. Surprised to see that he was not on the biggest of the group. He was on Oahu. The little world map to one side showed the group in the middle of the vast Pacific ocean. He suddenly felt very isolated. What the hell was he doing in the middle of the biggest ocean in the world? He figured it must be about two thousand miles before you got to America. Captain Cook showed up on the biggest island as a place with a bay. He suddenly realised how brave these explorers must have been. Wooden ships and only the stars to steer by. He traced the track that the blue line showed with his finger.

'Where are you my lovely teacher?'

Sunday

Saturday evening had not worked out well. They had both felt the impending split and it had coloured their time together. At the end of it all they had agreed to spend Sunday afternoon and evening together and then call it a day. Sunday afternoon came and Sam took the present he had bought for her out of his pocket the moment she walked into the Ala Moana bar.

'I bought you something to remember me by...' he almost added that it wasn't expensive but kept his mouth shut figuring that she would know it wasn't. She opened the little flat packet, no bigger than a playing card but too heavy for its size. The little cardboard card held a bronze coin set into its centre.

She read the print. 'A Waterhouse Token. What is a Waterhouse token?'

Sam heaved a sigh of relief. He had been afraid that she would have known all about it, just as she knew all about most other things.

'It's the first coin issued in Hawaii so that trade could take place. Thomas Waterhouse was a big business man and as he couldn't deal in coconuts or pineapples he issued his own money. Paid respect to the king, ' he leaned close to her catching the scent of her hair, ' see, 'His Majesty Kamehameha the forth'.'

She turned and kissed his lips. 'You're lovely.'

'Not lovely enough to keep in touch...'

'Too lovely to keep in touch. You see that don't you? Our different lives would cause so many problems. Imagine you deserted the army, how would you ever get to live in the US? I'm just starting out doing something I really love. Give it up and go to England, start over? Things get rocky and I end up blaming you; maybe hating you?' She reached out and stroked his cheek. 'It would take a miracle, no, three miracles to sort us out so nobody gets hurt. This is the best we will ever have.'

Sam saw what she meant. A mountain of problems that couldn't have been better arranged by a script writer for a sad film.

'You see into the future, something I never really do, something I'm not too good at,' he admitted, holding her hand to his cheek. 'Ok, deal. We say goodnight and go our separate ways. I have to be at Hickam for seven tomorrow morning so we say goodnight, when?' he gazed into her face hoping that she would not say now.

'Eleven,' she said, 'the eleventh hour.' Sam missed the point. 'Now,' she lifted the little present, 'A Waterhouse token?'

'Well I wanted to get you something that really meant Hawaii. As I've got so few dollars being at the end of my leave I thought anything I bought would be...' he hesitated, 'cheap; not right. Either too serious or too... cheap. I found this in the tourist office.'

'What were you doing in the tourist office? You haven't booked another two weeks holiday?' she laughed making him feel better.

'No. I went in to see where you had flown. Was it good?'

'Amazing. Volcanoes and beaches with black sand. If only...'

'Yeah. If only I was a millionaire. Anyway it's no good as money, it's out of date, from a different time...' he stopped again, 'like we will be after eleven o'clock.' The sob threatened just as it had in the cafe on Saturday.

She reached out and took his hand. 'Come on, there's dancing upstairs.'

'I can't dance.'

'Sure you can, you've got a certificate to prove it. Remember? Anyway this is slow dancing,' she smiled, her eyes sparkling, perhaps filled with tears. 'you just have to stand and sway. You can do that; stand, sway, hold me tight?'

They danced, walked late into the day then ate, drank and danced again. At eleven o'clock they kissed and said their final goodbye. Sam watched her as the lift doors closed then walked all the way back to the YMCA and lay weeping with a broken heart.

Back to work

The journey back to the island would have at one time been intensely interesting to Sam. Early breakfast at Hickam, the vast cafeteria lively and filled with the smells of coffee and sizzling bacon. Their kitbags stacked in the holding area of a vast hangar where they sat and smoked. Then the big silver Hastings on the runway, it's four engines idling gently. They boarded and found a seat; Robbie let Sam near the window still feeling fragile from the day before. The thrill of acceleration and the push of lifting off into the bright morning air. Watching the island of Oahu spread as the plane circled then grow smaller as the course was set, south to Christmas Island once more.

Sam saw it all with no interest. The light, the noise, the comments of his friends all seemed dulled, filtered through his total misery. All muted. Meaningless tableaux.

CHAPTER 14

A slow recovery

The sewerage Scheme

'We're on shit pits,' Sid welcomed them back to the island with this pleasantry. Sam groaned inwardly. From the Technicolor paradise with the loveliest woman in the world he felt as if he had fallen, like Lucifer, into the pit of hell. The shit pit of hell.

Once more he was in the flapping tent with the smell of diesel and sand, cigarette smoke and sweat. The place he felt he deserved. Sid went on to explain the next phase of the work which had started the week before. The aim was to build a sewerage system and then, once that was up and running the hutted camp could begin.

'What's that all about then?' Robbie wondered.

They sat in the Naafi. Geordie Thomson reached for the opener and levered two holes into his beer can. The flight back had been uneventful. The cloud of smoke that had ensued upon their exit from the plane had, Mickey Doyle imagined, alerted the Yanks to an unannounced bomb test. The arrival back in camp in time for tea had caused the usual questions. How many birds had you been able to shag? Was it easier if they were wearing a grass skirt?

The tale of Sam's adventures had been told a little distance down the tent as he had lain, as if mortally wounded, upon his bed. He had listened as they recounted the incident with the American girl and her boy friend. Had followed the description of the brawl and then launched into the story of Loretta and how she had rendered Sam so love struck that they assumed he would soon die of a broken heart. Mickey fluttered his hands to show Sam's soul leaving his wounded body. Sam listened in silence, his eyes closed as if asleep, the tears hot behind the lids.

'Not bad stuff, easy work,' Sid answered, 'laying concrete mostly at the moment. We're putting the bases down, twelve by twelve foot slabs to take the walls but you start from the bottom of a hole so that when you're finished the concrete box is buried below ground level and the control room sits on top. They look a bit like them concrete pill boxes you see all over the place back home.'

'How's it work then?'

'Fills up with sewage and then pumps it to the sewage farm,' Sid took a long drink.

'Gettin' bloody civilised round here,' Geordie grinned, 'we've only been away two weeks and the whole place is heading for pull chain bogs. Bet them RAF blokes'll be really pissed off losing their bonus for emptying Elsans!'

'No more camaraderie on the bog run then,' Robbie blew smoke and stubbed his State Express.

Tuesday morning saw Sam and the others being assigned tasks.

'Tamping and levelling, Smart, Hollingsworth.'

The concrete truck arrived and began pumping the concrete into the base. Geordie Thomson and Louis Patchittie spread the lava like stuff and Sam and Debbie Hollingsworth sawed and bumped it flat. The job was mindless, just what Sam wanted. He wondered why the lad on the other end of the plank was called Debbie. The only Debbie Sam knew was Debbie Renolds. Hollingsworth had blonde hair but that was where it finished, the rest of him was thin as tin. The sun climbed and sweat began to drip.

Back in hell thought Sam. What sort of a world is it that gives you something beautiful then snatches it away? He looked back on his life, Mum and Dad gone. He could barely remember Mum. She was more of a sensation than an image. She had raised him during the war with Dad away, first at Dunkirk then later, after getting back to England, on the Forts in the Mersey. He remembered her as slight, wrapped in a big dressing gown, its sleeves decorated with coloured cord sewn into a loop - like an admiral's badges of rank on the arm of his uniform. She was strict but not unkind. He would snuggle behind her on the nights when the raids were on. He never knew how she knew that he was picking his nose in the warm darkness. She would tell him to stop; an all seeing presence. At the end of the war she had died. He wondered how old she would be now. No idea.

Dad, a Scot from Aberdeen with a ready, easy sense of the funny, 'ha ha or peculiar, och I don't mind...' he would grin and blow smoke rings. His long ears pressed close to his head and his bull neck giving credence to his stories of boxing prowess. Alan Francis Steele Smart. Dad. Gone. Kicked in the chest by a lunatic at St John's Hospital Wandsworth when he was fifty five.

And now Loretta. Even her name was beautiful, exotic, not an Elsie or Doris, nor a hundred other ordinary names but Loretta. He said it gently, scarcely hearing the sound as he tamped the sluggish concrete into the shuttering; the noise of the pump breaking the beautiful name into tiny shards, broken crystal, each piece reflecting the high hot sun.

Plastering

'They're not waterproof is what!' corporal Chant answered the question that had followed the fact that there was more shit pit work to do.

'They're bloody solid concrete walls, bugger all would get through that, six inches thick!' Sid liked to assume the shop steward mantle, his size perhaps dictating that he should take care of the small guys who made up the squad.

'And porous,' the corporal added, 'nobody thought about the fact that we were using coral as aggregate, means that the walls soak it up like a sponge.'

'We're not going to have to build the fucking things all over again man?' Geordie Thompson squinted into the sun.

'No. We're going to plaster them.'

'I'm brilliant at plastering,' Geordie made sweeping movements.

'No. Getting plastered, different thing.' Robbie made drinking movements. Geordie told him to piss off.

Most of the pits had been finished and it was not until the first tests were carried out that the porous concrete was discovered. The coral was good for aggregate in most things but not if you wanted your concrete waterproof. Plastering looked to Sam to be a problem. The main chamber was underground with a manhole and iron ladder to get down in to it. The pill box on the top, ok control room as Lionel would have it, was just that, a square box with slits high up in the wall, a light, the pumping gear and a control panel. Again there was a doorway but no door.

'You'll be a bit cramped down in there,' Sam said.

'Not a lot of room for freedom of expression,' added Robbie.

'Us Geordies don't need much room. Remember we are mining stock. Born and bred at the coal face half a mile down and half a mile out to sea. Plastering in a shit pit... piece of piss,' he swept an imaginary float full of plaster against his imaginary wall. Sam wondered what it was like to be a miner.

'Fuck knows!' said Geordie, 'I worked in a factory.'

The only thing Sam knew about plaster was his experience with the sink plunger. He had discovered, while they were living in Tooting, that it could be flung against the wall in the bathroom after the fashion of a red Indian throwing a tomahawk and it would stick. The problem had occurred when he had unstuck it. A neat circle of plaster had come away with it. A white hole in the pale green painted bathroom wall. Tricky to explain such an accident. Dad had bought some plaster and smoothed it flat with a ruler. The circle remained as a memorial to Sam's skill with the tomahawk and the bollocking he had got.

The plaster arrived. The mixing board arrived. The floats, trowels and buckets arrived.

'Right Thompson, show us what you can do.' Corporal stood back in anticipation.

Geordie set to. Plaster dust whisked into the wind as he made the depression for the water he mixed frantically and finally shovelled a reasonable looking heap into the bucket. He picked up a float and a handled board and climbed down into the dark chamber.

'Smart, take the first bucket down and hold the lamp for the lad.' Sam climbed onto the ladder, Sid handed the bucket in nearly toppling Sam. Geordie loaded the board and skimmed the first float full onto the concrete wall. He loaded more onto the board and the first skim fell off.

'Shit, hold the fucking light steady.' Sam focussed the light holding it high, he felt like the statue of liberty but that reminded him of Loretta so he told Geordie that the 'fucking light ain't going to stick it on the wall!'

Geordie began retrieving the fallen plaster pushing it up the wall and watching it fall off.

'Too dry, we need to damp the wall first.'

Sam ordered a bucket of water and sloshed the wall. Geordie skimmed, the plaster slid off, much easier now that the wall was damp.

Corporal Chant started down the ladder.

'Nearly done? I'll get the lads to mix some more of the same... you haven't started. What you been doin' smoking?'

'It won't stick,' said Sam. Geordie still scooped plaster from floor to wall, ever more desperate that at least a small portion would remain in place, pushing it with his fingers. None did. Sam changed hands with the lamp.

'You have a go, Smart.'

'I can't plaster, corp...'

'Neither can he. Get cracking, you can't do any worse.'

Sam picked a fresh bit of wall. Dry. He scooped the first layer on and smoothed it. Then another scoop, another smooth. The plaster looked good, just a little touch there to get rid of the ridge. There.

'You're bloody good at this Smart, earned yourself a job...' The plaster slumped and slid to the floor.

'Bollocks!'

The morning wore on. Even Lionel couldn't get the stuff to stay on the wall. Sid tried brute strength and cut his knee with the float. Robbie tried science but ended up holding the mix against the wall unable to go further. Corporal Chant disappeared and turned up fifteen minutes later with Lieutenant Richards, Mr five percent.

'You've all had a go?' Lieutenant Richards was young, keen and very posh. He was obviously brainy being the man who summed up the amount of work done and thus the progress of the entire squadrons tasks. Thin, with a beak for a nose, Sam wondered if he had been picked for his looks and manner. He tended to dart about and his eyes were the best definition of beady that Sam had ever seen.

'All except Carr, Sir.'
'He's allergic or something?'
'No, just naturally clumsy.'
'I see.' The eyes beaded in on the corporal. 'Right. Tidy this lot up and take a break. I shall not be two ticks.' He stumped off across the site. The lads sloshed the tools off and lit up.

Fifteen minutes passed and Lieutenant Richards returned with a tall thin Sapper.
'Swales, from three eight squadron, he's a plasterer'.

The thin Bloke from three eight

Swales was even thinner than the lieutenant, gaunt and serious looking, he stood as if waiting to be introduced.
'Welcome to the land of people who can't stick plaster to walls,' said Robbie, 'Robbie Robinson, electrician.'
'Rog, Roger Swales...'
'Enough of the niceties,' corporal Chant broke in. 'Swales, you're in charge, we need this shit pit plastering, get on with it.'

The thin bloke from three eight certainly knew what he was up to. He showed them how to mix, climbed down with Sam into the chamber, got Sam to sweep up the loose plaster and propped the lamp up with a brush.
'Right, get mixing and keep it coming,' his final instruction as Sam hauled the first bucket load down. Sam watched in awe as the plaster began to cover the wall.
'Another bucket!' Swales shouted and Sam sped up the ladder.
'More plaster!'
'What! already?'
'Yeah, come on. He's going like a fucking train down there.'

Swales climbed the ladder. 'I can't plaster with no fucking plaster. I said, keep it coming!'

The production finally swung into action. Sam relayed the buckets.

'Christ that's quick,' he ventured at one point.

'Get paid by the yard in civvy street. More you do, more you get. You'd go mad taking your time. Best get on and get it done.'

'Why join the army then?'

'National service. No bloody choice. Why did you join the army?'

'Dad. No bloody choice.'

'Right. We've got to do the floor now. Work back to the ladder. Ready?'

Sam hauled more buckets and they backed their way across the floor then up the ladder.

The thin bloke from three eight did all the pits. The others took turns at mixing and buckets. Sam wondered about the national service. If he had carried on going to school, maybe even passed an exam or so, he would still have ended up in the army... or the navy? Did the navy do national service?

Twenty

The thirtieth of July came and Sam was twenty. He didn't mention it. Didn't feel like cake and candles, didn't feel like presents or even piss ups. 'Just become twenty and don't make a fuss,' he told himself. Robbie knew.

'Happy birthday, mate,' Robbie toasted him with a beer, as they wandered along the shore in the Saturday afternoon lull. They had finished for the day, Saturday morning being used to bull the tent up and prevent it from becoming a complete heap.

'How do you know it's my birthday?' Sam swigged his own beer and took a drag on his cigarette.

'Remembered it from that time back in training where I got pissed and you fell over...'

'Oh, yeah, right. embarrassing... nuff said.'

'Anyway,' Robbie picked up the conversation, 'you have to get sorted. You are never going to see Loretta again not even if you eventually quit the army and put an add in a Washington news paper. By that time she would have moved on, become a head mistress and married a Yank...'

'Yeah, OK. I get the picture. I suppose you're right. She just fills all my thinking. She's always there, sneaks up on me first thing in the morning when I open my eyes. Sits beside me at breakfast, says good night to me when I go to bed. She leaves me useless, fucking useless...'

'Precisely. You'll mope yourself into an early grave for something that's never going to change.'

'So what do I do?'

'I don't know mate, but you've got to do something or you'll go under. There's a bloke in the signals got a dear John from his bird back in Blighty and he tried to kill himself. Took a whole load of aspirin or something. Another bloke, same thing, dear John went round all his mates collecting photo's of other birds, put them in a parcel and posted them to her telling her to take the ones of her out and send the rest back...'

'No!'

'Well I didn't think so either, not many blokes would give you a picture of their bird to be sent off and probably never come back. Good story though. What I'm getting at is that these two did daft things to get over the loss. Why not just accept that the outcome is the outcome. If you burn your finger no amount of swearing at the fire will make it any better. Like my mum used to say, 'you'll get over it,' that's the trick, get over it.'

Sam tried. Sometimes he succeeded, sometimes he failed but gradually his victories began to outstrip the failures. The month moved on, August twenty second saw a ground test. A bomb set off from a balloon.

CHAPTER 15

More bombs

The ground test

'Trigger devices' said Pete Cunningham as they sat in the tent. He knew all about them. 'Naturally', thought Sam. Where he got all this info was a mystery. The round framed glasses and his oval face gave him something of a Japanese look but that was spoiled by his frizzy ginger hair. Still, he was a useful source of information to them all.

'So, what's a trigger thingy then?' Big Sid handed the ciggies round.

'A trigger device is used to set off a hydrogen bomb' Pete accepted a light

'Right,' said Sam, realising the answer begged even more questions but deciding against asking them.

'So this next one is a trigger device which goes off from a balloon or a tower and Mickey and Jim have been chosen for generator duties.'

'That's right,' Jim Hayward put Sam's guitar down for a moment, 'so what the fuck are generator duties? They didn't tell us a thing. Just report for generator duties.'

'Piece of piss,' Pete grinned, 'You zoom in before it goes off and switch on the generators which have been installed in deep pits. Then you sandbag them up with just the air supplies open and then shift like greased shit out of there. Boom goes the bomb and you wait two hours then zoom back in, whip the sandbags off and shut down the gennys. Easy.'

'What if a bit of the bomb hasn't gone off?' Tommy wanted to know.

'We ain't talking gun cotton here,' said Pete, 'Once the explosion has happened there's nothing left, no balloon, no tower, nothing just glassy sand and white marker rocks. They show you where the gennys are. The landscape is totally different when you go back.'

'Bloody hell!' Jim picked up the guitar again and played a surprisingly good bit of Spanish Flamenco sounding music, his face thoughtful, the cigarette slack between his lips.

Sam reckoned Jim could have been a film star. He was good looking piled on thick. Square jaw, regular features, eyes blue as a summer sky and yet dark hair that looked good even with the short army cut. Sam had met Jim in Erlestoke wondering whether to buy a guitar but finally leaving it too late - possibly on purpose - getting Sam to haul the Voss half way round the world so he could learn in peace. He had a sense of humour enjoying the ridiculous. Coming back from town on the bus one night Jim had said he was tired and propped his eyelids open with matchsticks. The pair had hooted with laughter all the way back to camp particularly when a bubble of mucus had popped out of Jim's straight handsome nose. 'Disgusting!' they had both chorused and laughed all the more.

The advantage and problem of being Jim's companion on their evenings out was simple: Jim attracted girls in droves. He would walk across the dance floor, ask a stunning blonde to dance. She would sparkle and smile and take not a blind bit of notice of the invisible Sam. The small mercy was that he had never fancied Jill. Sam would have found that heartbreaking even given the fact that he was too frightened to approach the girl. Jill had been a bit of Loretta really. He put the thought away.

'Anyway,' Pete Cunningham continued, ' With this one you won't get so much bloody Jazz.

'That's a shame,' said Lionel from the other end of the tent.

More Jazz

As it turned out there was jazz.

'Chuffed to bits!' Lionel happy was a rare thing. Lionel thoughtful behind his camera was the norm. The camera with the Wrayflex Lens that they had all been shown at great length. Sam had marvelled along with the others that a camera should come with it's lens in a separate, silk lined box. They cooed their interest and made Lionel happy. But now it was the jazz, he really loved jazz.

There was the usual march to the sand grass area, the only difference being that Mickey Doyle and Jim had grabbed their packs and vanished early to do the mysterious 'generator duties.'

'Why do they need generators?' Yorkie Carr had wondered.

'There's loads of stuff that needs a supply just to set the device off,' Lionel called it a device, to everyone else it was a bomb, 'and then there's the TV cameras.'

'Is it on TV?' Tommy lit a fag, 'I could have stayed home and watched it instead of being cast away on a fucking desert island with no birds.'

'There's frigate birds,' Sam stirred the conversation a little.

'Totty, you twat!' Tommy had a poets ear for words.

'The TV cameras are close to the device and they record the first few milliseconds of the explosion in ultra slow motion. As the TV signal moves the same speed as the flash it is always just ahead and can be filmed in super high speed. Brilliant lenses and about twenty miles of film...'

'What happens to the TV cameras then?' Sid poured himself some tea from his flask.

'They melt...'

'Well that's fucking useless...'

'No, like I said, the pictures are always just in front of the fireball. All recorded by the time the cameras melt.

Sam struggled with the idea as they sat cross legged in the sand grass.

'We could try that seeing the flash trick,' he said, 'you know, the fists like binoculars thing.'

'You going to have a go then?' Sid screwed his big hands into fists as if adjusting the focus.

'Yeah.' Sam squinted through his 'fist bino's' looking down at the coarse grass that grew through the coral sand.

Watson's hat

Mickey Doyle came back late in the afternoon and joined Sam, Robbie, Sid and Tommy on the wicker chairs looking out over the ocean.

'Genny duties take a bit of time,' Sid pressed his vast frame into the chair making it creak ominously, 'you've been gone since half past nine.'

'Watson's fault,' Mickey lit a fag, 'got himself radio active, silly sod.'

At the mention of radioactivity they all moved forward. The sea broke against the reef and they leaned in to hear about Watson

'Didn't get blown up then?' Tommy wondered.

'No, it was his hat.'

'His hat got blown up?' Sam wondered how you just got your hat blown up. Could be useful if he ever got posted to a war zone.

'Hang on and I'll tell you,' Mickey took a long drag on his ciggy and thanked Sid for the proffered can of beer. 'First thing we had to do was turn the genny's on and get them running smooth. Once that was done then we sandbagged them up against blast and got out quick to the next one. Watson, tall bloke, mechanic from three eight, dropped his hat while we were sandbagging, couldn't get down to it with us lot going like stink to get it done so had to leave it. He had a great hat, almost bleached white and shaped like one of them alpine trilbies. The brim had really shrunk.'

The thing about hats was that when they were issued they looked stupid. Big floppy brim, olive green with a totally shapeless crown. As with all military hats the first duty of any squaddie was to get it into shape, his idea of shape. As a boy soldier Sam had slashed his peak - cut the stitching either side of the half moon of peak so that it could be pushed back closer to the forehead - making you look less like a postman. Next you put a pole, either bent cardboard or an ice lolly stick, behind the front to push the top of the hat higher. More like a German general than a first world war Tommy. Then you soaped the top and 'spun' it with a brush to create that disc like sheen normally seen on the top hats of the aristocracy.

Berets were easier, just shrink and shape to the head. The Olive Green monstrosity that was tropical issue needed to be shrunk and bleached then shaped with the brim curling up; jaunty, a bit like a Newmarket bookie's hat.

So the loss of a well shaped hat was really something. Sam and the others commiserated.

'The point was,' Mickey continued, 'that when we came back to uncover the gennys and shut them down he finds his hat and pops it on his head.'

'Lucky that,' said Sid.

'No,' Mickey paused dramatically, 'It's radioactive!'

'But still a good hat.'

Sam thought that Sid was perhaps missing a point here. He could imagine the hat glowing, like the luminous watch faces that showed up in war films. He had heard somewhere that they were radioactive. Maybe a luminous hat could be useful. Reading in bed after lights out maybe.

'No, listen,' Mickey continued, 'We were wearing paper suits to avoid getting radioactive sand on us and they were taken off in the decontamination tent and got burned. Watson troops through for a Geiger reading and it goes off the scale! Everything has to be checked, we all have to shower in case we've picked up some and Watson gets his hat destroyed and was still in the shower when I left. And he had to have some jollop to flush his insides out.'

'So, all of you genny duties mob have been radioactived?' Tommy leaned back in his chair. Sam could hear the cockney cogs working. 'All that area is radioactive?'

'I reckon so. It's fenced off and out of bounds to squaddies. Only scientists allowed in to monitor the levels. I'll tell you something else,' Mickey took a swig of beer, 'there's a patrol goes out to catch fish so that they can keep an eye on the sea and another patrol shoots blind birds.'

'Fucking hell!' Tommy stopped his cogitating. 'Shoot blind birds. How'd they get blind?'

'The flash. They don't know a bomb is going off and so, if they are close enough and looking toward the bomb, they get blinded. They're easy to spot, they don't take off when you get near them. Good eyesight rotten hearing.' Mickey dropped the stub of his smoked ciggy into the empty beer can.

'Poor buggers.' The soft side of Tommy; left pensive by Mickey's tale and sorry for a frigate bird.

Aldershot

The shit pits were done. Well they were done as far as Sam and the others were concerned. Robbie and the pump people could get them working. 'Funny,' Sam thought, 'that the job on the pumping stations should finish on the twenty fourth of August. He had started his army service on that day in nineteen fifty three. Easy day to remember.

Dad's discovery of his truancy meant that he had to follow his father's 'advice' which boiled down to you will do as I say and join the forces. Each force was tried. The RAF examination paper may as well have been a university application. Meaningless as far as Sam was concerned. The Navy and the Army apprentices equally baffled him. It began to dawn on him that he had avoided the fate worse than... well, being in the forces and he had inwardly felt a surge of excitement and expectation until the sergeant said 'Your Son could of course take a simple intelligence test for the Royal Engineers Boys Service.'

'Shit!' thought Sam.

The old sergeant in charge of the intelligence test was bald and Irish with a gentle brogue obviously designed to pacify anxious fifteen year olds. The little office with the folding table and single chair was so still he could hear the man breathe. The paper and pen were placed in front of him and he was asked to begin.

'How many half penny stamps can you buy for five pence?' the first question asked. Sam wondered if a completely stupid answer might complete his fait accompli and keep him forces free for the rest of his life, when he heard the intake of breath that preceded 'If you get stuck don't worry, I know all the answers. Can't have you looking silly can we?' The Irishman smiled. Sam wrote 'ten' and joined the army.

He had a medical in Croydon and signed the papers under the stern eye of his Father. He listened to Uncle Reg, stepmum Grace's brother, give advice from his army days.

'Aldershit we called it. Red caps, military police, at every corner. Put your hands in your pockets and you got shot. You'll love it.'

One way ticket.

And so he got off the train at Aldershot at one o'clock on the twenty fourth of August nineteen fifty three. The sun shone brightly with big clouds looming all around threatening thunder. Following the map he had been given he set off, past the NAAFI club and up Gun hill. The Army pervaded everything. He changed his little case from hand to hand to avoid slipping into his old habit of putting his hand in his pocket. The fact that every Hollywood leading man seemed to keep one hand firmly thrust into his trouser pocket did not help.

At the top of the hill the heavens opened and rain lashed down through the strong sunlight. Big spots that splashed into his space beneath the sheltering tree. The gutters rushed then the rain was gone and he continued toward the barracks.

'Sit down lad,' the sergeant directed him to a long ledge, it could not be described as a seat. Built of brick, part of the wall itself, the base was whitewashed while the top was painted glossy black. This was the guard room. Windows looked out onto a vast parade ground bounded on three sides by tree lined roads. The one opposite busy with traffic, a tall steepled church on the far side. Sam knew from his map that this was Queens Parade and the church was the garrison church. He sat in silence. The sergeant stood gazing across the parade ground. A short chubby lad arrived and gave his name as Thomas Fullick. He sat down next to Sam saying nothing, as if afraid. A truck arrived and a bunch of youngsters jumped down and came into the room. The sergeant ticked their names off.

'Dancey, Steve Dancey.' A broad faced blond lad introduced himself to Sam. They shook hands.

'Keep quiet! It's not a cocktail party,' the sergeant silenced them all and ordered them outside shifting them into two ragged lines. A corporal appeared and ordered them to face right and follow him. They set off, not in step, not smartly, a ragged, ill assorted bunch that seemed to conform to no type other than they were all fifteen years old.

The barrack room stood one floor up in the red brick Victorian building, one of maybe six, that comprised the Gibraltar Barracks complex. Again the black gloss paint, again the whitewash and now and dark green gloss paint that covered the bottom half of the wall. Beds and lockers along each wall between the tall windows. Sam chose a bed toward the end of the room, the window looking out over a small parade square. He dumped his suitcase on the bare steel bed. 'Another convent bed,' he thought

'Outside!' The first shouted order of his army career. Again they formed up and followed the corporal to the bedding stores. A thin mattress, four blankets, two sheets a pillow and pillowcase were issued. The corporal showed them how to roll the bedding into the mattress and hoist it onto their shoulders. They struggled, still in formation, back to the barrack room. The narrow stairs brought the first laughter of the day as they hauled the loose bundles up to the room above.

'Make your beds, five minutes then Outside again.' They made their beds.

The next stop was the stores for their kit. First world war surplus. Brass buttoned khaki tunic, peaked cap with chinstrap and hat badge nestling inside. Brushes, belts, boots and a button stick. Shirts, socks, laces, plimsolls, pants, vests. Mess tins, knife fork and spoon, mug. A lanyard and then, mysteriously, a sheet of brown paper and a length of string. They struggled back to the barrack room and again stowed the kit as best they could.

The armoury provided Lee Enfield rifles. The pay office pay books, part one and part two, one brown the other cream.

Numbers had been entered, names written in. They signed the forms.

At last they seemed to have reached the end. The room began to fill with tentative conversation. What's this? Why that? Where're you from? Dancey put his hat on backward and aimed his rifle

'Won't know wevver I'm comin, or goin' His cockney accent familiar to Sam.

'They'll still shoot you, whack!' a tall thin faced lad grinned from the other end of the room' This was, Sam later discovered, Scouse Downey. Even later he discovered that Scouse was not his first name but merely an indicator that he came from Liverpool. Dad had been at Liverpool. Sam liked the lad right away.

Sergeant Vivash

'Stand by your beds!'

Sergeant Vivash introduced himself shouting his name.

'Sergeant is my first name, Vivash is my last name and bastard is my middle name. Tomorrow is haircuts,' at this he swept his beret off to reveal his head shorn almost clean of hair. His powerful body and bull neck made his head look small, the beret almost an afterthought.

'This evening is learning. Pay book part one,' he produced one from his pocket, 'That number on the inside is your army number. You will learn that ready for parade tomorrow morning.' He picked a rifle from Tom Fullick's bed and pointed out the number on the breech. 'Your rifle number, you will learn that as well. Clear?' They all said yes and nodded.

'Yes sergeant!' he bellowed 'Yes sergeant.' they mimicked.

'Lastly you will notice that you have a sheet of brown paper and a piece of string. That is to wrap your civvies in and send home. Understand?' The yes sergeant was shouted back.

'Right. Eating irons and mugs, then outside. Time for tea. Breakfast is at seven tomorrow morning. So the twenty forth of August nineteen fifty three was completed and now, twenty forth of August nineteen fifty eight saw the completion of the shit pits.

CHAPTER 16

Work

Life goes on.
 The work on the pits had been heavy and suddenly there seemed nothing to do, always a danger sign in the army, Sam had learned. They would find you something to fill the hours and sure enough Sam and Robbie were set the task of camp tidying.
 'What a waste of a qualified electrician! he wailed, 'farting about moving junk and re-arranging forty gallon drums!'
 'Can't really complain can we,' Sam took a more measured view, 'as we are just farting about nobody knows what the fuck we are up to, how much we have done, how much we have to do. All we have to do is make sure that Kenty, our all seeing sergeant, thinks we are busy. Rest of the time wander about smoking.'
 The routine dragged and threatened to tip Sam back into thoughts about Loretta.
 Terry Ogilvy sat on the next bed reading a letter from home.
 'Bit here for you Sam, I told my bird about your Hawaiian adventure. She reckons the only cure for a broken heart is to find a new bird...'
 'Bit difficult on this island,' Sam nodded to indicate the island, 'Mable and Doris are spoken for.'
 'Whose Mable and Doris?' Yorkie Carr never tired of listening in to any conversation that was going.
 'WVS ladies,' Sam told him.
 'Never knew you knew their names...'
 'He doesn't, you twat, he's having you on.' Tommy Marks joined the conversation.

'Anyway,' Terry continued, 'She's got a mate called Jean who wouldn't mind being a pen friend. Says if I ask you and you say yes she'll send you a letter.'

'What if she's ugly?'

'She's not. I met her once, blonde, OK. Works in a shop.'

Sam really didn't have to think hard about this one. The idea of a girl taking an interest in him, aged twenty, far from home with not a bird in sight really didn't make the choice difficult.

'Yeah, all right. Tell her I'll write back if she writes.'

'OK.'

Clearing

A bull dozer came rumbling across the sand where they had all gathered.

'Not more bloody roads,' Tommy Marks spoke for them all.

'No, Marks. A storage area,' sergeant Kent indicated the area now being crossed by the dozer. 'flat as a pancake and laid out in orderly blocks so that we can take delivery of your loverly, luxurious 'uts. Four concrete bases which you lot are good at.'

'How much concrete do you reckon we have mixed and laid on this fucking island?'

Sam reckoned Tommy's question was a good one. 'But,' he pointed out, 'we haven't covered it all yet. Still sand all round our tents.' He remembered the joke about the three paddies arriving in the Sahara desert and wanting to get out quick 'before the fooking cement arrives!'

The concrete was laid. The trucks began to arrive. The team unloaded heavy boxes of nuts and bolts, small but impossible to lift. Rollers were brought in and the crates slid from the truck to the stand. Stacks were created. Stacks of soft board and hard board. Stacks of timber panels, windowless for the hut ends; and finally they watched as big low loaders arrived with roof trusses bundled together like the ribs of some vast wooden ship. Wall panels packed like books, the glassless windows already built in making tunnels through the stack. The huts had arrived.

The hutted camp

While Sam and the others had been busy with the vast storage area, so others had been busy laying out the concrete slabs that would become the foundations for the huts. Suddenly the layout became visible, giant footsteps in the sand. 'The lines', as military parlance would have it. The streets began to appear, floors were laid and walls began to be erected. Sam was teamed up with Robbie on wiring.

'Told you I'd get you a job as a sparks,' Robbie boasted but Sam reckoned it was more down to canny choosing, as Geordie would have it, mates worked better with mates. They measured lengths, marked drums of electric wire, collected clips and fuse boxes, light fittings and wall sockets. Once the walls were up and the roof trusses in place then they began to thread the cables along the top of the walls. Robbie notched the beginning of each wire then Sam would thread it through the building to its final destination. Robbie would cut and notch the other end to match. The sun beat down through the uncovered roof and the two men whistled as they worked, hoisting their stepladders about noisily.

Sam had always enjoyed whistling. He couldn't really remember a time when he had not whistled. Uncle Henry, Grace's brother, had sung. A tall, florid man he had a fine tenor voice and would sing opera at family gatherings. Sam was no singer but enjoyed the music and sought out the recordings from Henry's collection. The music transported him. He would sway and conduct, a foible he learned from Henry who also told him the stories hidden in the opera's Italian librettos. Later he would whistle the same pieces as he did the washing up after the evening meal, the window over the sink being open in the summer and so Sam whistling to an unseen audience. To the world the whistling probably sounded plaintive, a thin shimmer of sound but to the whistler, who could hear the violins, cellos, brass and percussion of the original it sounded so marvellous he would sometimes cry.

Later on he whistled tunes from the wireless, popular songs, light opera and marches. These marches were Robbie's particular favourites and gave both men the opportunity to show off the accompanying trills and flutters usually played on the fife or flute. The site grew to whistling and hammering and the clatter of boots on newly laid floors. The maze of walls and openings encouraged ingenuity.

Hunger.

At an average age of twenty the workforce could be counted hungry at any moment other than the end of a meal and that was not always guaranteed if the main course had been particularly tasty: seconds were not readably available.

'Watch,' Tommy marks banged his table knife into the top of the little tin of baked beans then carefully began to work the blade around the edge using the squared back of the blade against the raised rim of the tin. With care he began to open the top. 'easy.' He forked the cold beans into his mouth and tossed unopened cans to the others who sat having their morning tea break in one of the half constructed huts.

'Can't you use your jack knife for this?' Yorkie Carr experimented.

'It's OK for the first bit but the blade's too wide for the opening movement.' Tommy had obviously tried this.

'Where'd you get the beans?' Sid had his can opened and spooned beans up hungrily.

'Cook house,' Tommy replied.

Sam remembered breaking into the cookhouse in Gibraltar barracks, him and Steve Dancy and another... he couldn't remember now. He did remember the dim kitchen smelling of yeast. So many cabbages, potatoes, carrots but nothing that would satisfy the hunger of sixteen year old boy soldiers. Then Steve had found the tray of Yorkshire pudding. Cold and not yet cut into squares it had rolled up easily. A big tin of jam from the shelf and they had run back to the barrack room. Yorkshire pudding and apricot jam; the taste was with him still.

Eventually Lionel asked how he had managed it. Tommy touched the side of his nose with his finger and said nothing. The mystery deepened when Tommy asked Robbie to get an old cement drum next time he was collecting cable rolls. One was found and brought back to the hut jungle. As Tommy had specified the top was still attached by a bit of un-chopped metal. He took delivery and hauled the drum off.

The whisper went round that breakfast would be served on a rolling basis.

'I had breakfast at seven,' Robbie noted'

'And me,' added Sam. They went to see and found Tommy cooking bacon and sausages on the modified cement drum. Tommy had cut it in half and dented the sides in to support the shallow saucer of the lid. Holes had been punched in the side and a fire of coconut husks burned hot within. A loaf of sliced bread stood ready for sandwich making.

'You'll be in the shit if anyone finds out,' Sam thought it only fair to point this out as he munched on a sausage wrapped in bread. 'did you get any onions?'

'It's a mid morning snack not a main meal you twat,' Tommy forked bacon out for Sid and Robbie. 'Anyway, who's going to tell? You know when anyone's coming round, just give the shout and...' he indicated two steel jumping bars, 'slide these through and carry the whole lot out the back. Nothing to it.'

'They'll get red hot,' Yorkie Carr pointed out.

'Well you don't leave them in there and you ain't gonna be running for miles. Just out of sight. What do you think?'

'I think it's bloody marvellous,' said Sid.

'Shit hot idea,' said Micky Doyle.

And so midmorning tea break became civilised.

Mr Five Percent

The huts were easy. Once a couple had been built the routine became mechanical. The corrugated aluminium arrived for the roofs. The site was filled with the sound of hammering and Louis Patchitti became the first man to fly.

Mr five percent, lieutenant Richards, made a visit to the building site about every other day or so. Considering the area he had to cover, unknown to Sam and the others, he did very well striding in with his clip board clutched to his chest lest the breeze ruffle his papers too much. On these days the lookout system had to be particularly vigilant so as to move the 'moveable feast', as Lionel called it, beyond his sight.

'These three blocks completely wired and fittings in.' Robbie showed the lieutenant his handiwork. Sam trailed on behind ready to nip off and warn should the tour take a wrong turning. Lieutenant Richards had a habit of darting off if he spotted something that could go down on his lists. They moved on down the partially completed huts. 'Wired, lights and sockets in progress. Two more units not complete enough for wiring,' Robbie indicated the partially built huts further down the line. Lieutenant Richards darted forward and Sam slipped between the huts and ran down to the where Tommy was getting tea break ready. He readied the iron bars but as they watched lieutenant Richards turned to the opposite block and began counting percentages, scribbling figures in, the string on the pencil end dancing in the breeze . Sam crept back and joined them.

'Funny thing, Robinson; it is Robinson is it?'
'Yes Sir.'
'Funny thing the trade wind...' he paused. Robbie waited. Lieutenant Richards looked about him and squinted up into the sun. 'We must be, what, about half a mile from the cookhouse which lies over there,' he pointed with his clip board, the leaves ruffling in the breeze, he smoothed them, 'and the wind is blowing from the north west I should say,' he checked the sun again, 'which is about ninety degrees off from the direction of the cookhouse and yet I can smell bacon cooking as if the place were next door...'

'We get that all the time,' said Robbie quickly, 'drives us mad sometimes when it's a particularly strong smell and we are hungry. We reckon it has to do with the part built walls, causing the wind to flurry about, back on itself in a circle as it were.' He stirred the wind with his hand as he spoke.

'Yes... good theory that. Interesting. Yes...' he checked his clip board and glanced once more up into the sun, 'Good theory Robinson. Carry on.' Sam and Robbie saluted and lieutenant Richards strode off back the way he had come.

'Time for a bacon butty me thinks,'
'Too right,' said Sam, 'while the wind's in the right direction.' They trudged off toward Tommy's mobile kitchen and Louis Patchitti landed in front of them, seated on a sheet of corrugated aluminium.

CHAPTER 17

Play

Flying

'Bloody hell!' the shout went up around them with the loudest shout coming from Louis himself. His hat landed beside him and he pushed at his short black hair to knock the white coral sand from it. He spat twice and got to his feet, clearly shaken.

'Silly sod,' Robbie was all heart, 'what you want to do that for? Scared the shits out of us and nearly broke your neck into the bargain...'

'You dinna think I did it on purpose,' Sam could see Louis was upset, his Scottish accent coming to the fore, 'I thought it was fixed and so I moved onto it to do the next one and the fucking thing took off! Jeez. Slid down the roof. Thought I was dead then it just flew!'

'Good landing mate,' Johnny Keene came up and examined the sheet of aluminium with a practised eye. Johnny was a nice bloke, a round moon of a face with a ready smile. Rumour had it that he had been flung into the army because he had nicked a car. A bit more serious than bunking off school but the punishment the same. He certainly loved driving. 'Give us a wheelie,' was his request when ever any new transport came into play. Scrapers, dumper trucks, lorries even the bulldozer were driven with ease by the cheeky Londoner. He just seemed built to be at the wheel of something. He wandered off with the aluminium sheet. Louis allowed himself to be fussed over.

Robbie and Sam remembered the sausages cooking two huts along. There was a whoop behind them and they turned to see Johnny Keene just landed on the aluminium sheet amid a cloud of dust.

'Silly sod,' said Sam and continued toward the sausages.

Flying looked like becoming a craze until Jim Hayward came a cropper. His magic carpet took the short way down! Jim might just as well have jumped off the roof.

'Weight distribution, that's the thing,' Lionel pointed out that if you were too heavy the magic carpet effect didn't work. Jim rubbed his knees but managed to stand up and stagger off.

Saturday afternoon

Saturday afternoons were like that on Christmas Island; nothing to do but wait for Saturday evening! Sam took himself up the beach for a bit of peace and quiet The constant breeze, the constant flapping of canvas, the constant... companionship? Natter? Always somebody talking. He supposed he should be pleased to be surrounded by mates but sometimes it was nice to be quiet. He sat down in the shade and leaned against the round trunk of a palm tree. Most of the others were either asleep or swimming and always there was a football game in progress. Now he sat alone watching the waves break over the reef a hundred yards or so off. A team from three eight had blasted a gap through it and laid the sewage outfall pipes. The pits, the huts, the whole camp getting plumbed into this once innocent desert island. He suddenly caught the vastness and the smallness of it all. He remembered looking at a globe some chap had got hold of. If you turned it so that Christmas Island was in the middle of your view then you could see only the fringes of the continents around the edges of the globe, all else was ocean.

'Good place to test bombs,' he thought, 'bad place to be if something goes wrong.'

September had seen two more tests. Out on the sandgrass they sat through the jazz and Tannoy sessions for one aircraft drop on the eleventh and a balloon detonation on the twenty third. Same jazz, same jokes, same squinting at the flash through squeezed up fists with the warm, electric fire glow against your back. Everything had taken on a terrible sameness. Nothing new.

He lit a cigarette and blew smoke into the insistent breeze. Land crabs crept among the dead palm fronds, the long line of surf broke white against the distant reef. Sam saw Loretta teaching in school, her blonde hair a perfect bell about her face, her slight figure outlined against the black board. The autumn term. He wondered what the weather was like in Washington; here on the island there were no seasons just constant high, bright sun and the trade wind.

His thought changed. He thought of Jill in Trowbridge, again the blonde bell of hair framing her pale face. Where was she now? Still in Trowbridge? Would he go there when he got home, find her? The two girls merged, Loretta had now outshone her, like the flash from the bomb - so bright leaving no shadows. Her bright invisible light. He flicked the butt of his cigarette into the sand and watched as a crab picked it up in its large claw.

'That won't fill you up mate,' the crab dropped it and stared at Sam in silent agreement.

'Enough.' He got up and walked back along the beach to where the lads were sitting on the old cane chairs. No one had any idea how the cane furniture had arrived. It was certain that it had not been transported at great cost across the world for the use of lowly squaddies like themselves. The best opinion had it that it was thrown out of the officers mess when a more luxurious set had arrived. Benny, the Fijian soldier, had joined Robbie, Sid and Scouse and was in the midst of a great laughing fit. That was Bennie, he never stopped smiling or laughing. They still fooled about on the guitar, singing. He had a rich deep voice and an incredible sense of rhythm. He would supply the bass line to Louis Patchitti's higher voice.

'Benny's wondering about football,' Sid took a swig from his can of Tennants, 'reckons he'd be good at it.'

'Daft game,' Sam still didn't understand the passion the game aroused, 'massive great goal,' he said, 'and little thin goalie in a cap. Boof! Goal! Load of bollocks.

'Ah but,' Scouse joined in, 'getting the ball just in the right position so the boof can happen, there's the skill. You should have a go, mate, you'd enjoy it.'

The conversation flagged. They sat waiting for Saturday evening. Benny heaved himself out of the flimsy cane chair, knocking it over.

'Don't worry, I take a photo of you all, show my mumma what you look like. Tell her the chairs are too little, ha!'

'Red Leister!'

'Cheddar!'

Unable to think of a cheese Sam just watched the camera lens having been told once that it would make the photograph somehow more personal.

Then the sound happened; faint against the breeze, nothing more than the distant cry of a bird, an almost casual sound that happened once more and then again revealing its true, life hungry urgency.

'Happy days are here again!' A cynical shout from one of the other tables, 'someone's over the reef!'

The Reef

'Bloody hell!' Robbie stubbed his cigarette and stood up shading his eyes looking out to the ocean, beyond the line of surf.

'There!' Benny pointed, walking to the waters edge. 'Swim out!' he shouted toward the distant figure. He began pushing with his arms as if he would push the swimmer out into the vast Pacific ocean.

'Swim out! Keep tellin' him that, signal to swim out. He comes in he get lifted up and smashed, tell him swim out.'

Benny took his shorts off and knelt to tie his plimsolls tight pulling on the laces and tying a double knot.' Call the Raff to come and get us.'

Scouse ran off toward the guardroom. Sam watched the big Fijian as he waded out toward the reef. Now he could see him clearly, dark against the white breakers, lifting his arms, filling his lungs, moving left and right.

'What's he looking for?' Robbie stood beside Sam both of them shielding their eyes from the sun.

'A gap,' Sam said. 'He told me once about launching a canoe from Fiji, he needs a gap.' As if on cue Benny suddenly crouched, almost like a runner in the blocks the spume of a wave almost toppling him and then he launched himself into the spent, rushing, retreating wave. Sam watched as the big Fijian was sucked away amid the swirling, heaving water. Then he was gone. The ocean became once more the distant Pacific. No sign of Benny, no sign of the swimmer who had cried out.

Scouse came back. 'The raff are on to it. Just got to get the helicopter going. Where they go?'

'Out to sea.'

'Maybe the sharks have got them,'

'Fucking hell Rob...!'

'Shark comes near Benny he'll kill it...' Sid jutted his chin. 'Helicopter's taking its time!'

'Takes a while to get the thing started, and the crew to get their kit on.' Scouse cupped his eyes and scanned the empty ocean. It seemed quiet once more, the boring Saturday afternoon stillness all around, as if nothing had happened, as if nature had not noticed their little emergency.

'Hey! look out there, way out; fer Christ's sake what's he doing?'

Beyond the troughs, maybe six waves out Benny rose with the swimmer clutched to his chest, his arm swimming them both relentlessly out.

'They'll be in Hawaii at that rate if the helicopter don't show up soon,' Scouse waved and to his surprise both men waved back as the helicopter flew into view, the D net swinging below ready to scoop them both up.

They went back to their drinking. Benny didn't come back; they guessed he would be with the MO getting the once over.

Benny was the hero of the hour in the NAAFI that night. He showed off the bandage on his lower leg where the coral had gashed him. They drank, ate hamburgers and piled the cans high in the tower building competitions. Benny and the Fijians sang and told outrageous stories of south sea island life. Benny told those that would listen that he was 'gonna be a footballer'.

'Soon as this is healed I'm gonna sign up for a team.' Surprising what a drop of beer can do.

Football?

The game on the island was a mystery to Sam. Never interested, he did not begrudge the football fans their fun but often wondered what they could see in it. Not only football but cricket and a host of other ball games left him blank. Sure, he could understand the pleasure in hitting a ball or punting a football into a goal. The same sort of pleasure one might get from skimming a stone for three bounces across a placid lake. But again and again? Surely the excitement would fade?

Jackie Bones and Chic Brown were the football men. Sam had watched them in the NAAFI answering questions, almost a memory man double act. He had met Chick back at Erlstoke. Glasgow Razor boy they all said. The same height as Sam but with a hardness in his construction. You felt that if you hit him you would hurt your fist rather than hurting him. His hair was the palest blond and his eyes a piercing blue. He drank a lot like most Scotsmen Sam had yet known and they had met, crucially, while Sam was on guard.

The little sentry box housed only one, and afforded a bit of protection against the Wiltshire wind and rain. The last bus would stop at the gate to discharge it's drunken passengers and the guard, on this night Sam, would wave them all benignly in.

'Y' wannin' a drink pal?' Chick leaned into the box and offered a bottle of brown ale, breathing fumes over Sam. The top was still on so it seemed safe to take it for later on. The fact that Chick was a menacing presence helped the decision. The man instilled fear just by his pale blue eyed blondness. Smile or no smile you knew you could be in trouble. Sam took the bottle with a thank you and stood wondering what the next move would be. Chick leaned heavily against the box, breathing deeply as if to ward off a dizzy spell. Would he spew? All the other bus passengers had gone into camp, Sam could hear their occasional whoops as they headed to bed.

'Hey! s'no open,' Chick took the bottle and uncapped it with his teeth, a single confident movement as if opening it on a metal bar opener.

'There... cheers...' he handed the bottle to Sam and produced another from his pocket. The same single movement opened his and he took a deep swig.

Drinking on duty is a punishable offence. Sam figured that refusing a drink with a supposed Glaswegian razor boy would also incur some comeback. He swigged deeply and determined to light a ciggy as soon as possible.

The ending was quite tame really, Chick had taken the bottle from him so that he wouldn't be caught drinking and had wished him good night. From that time on he had become a sort of friend, always a smile, always a joke. Sam grew to like him and guessed that the hard man image was perhaps a baseless but useful front among fellow soldiers. He wondered whether it was because Dad came from Scotland.

'Brave as a lion,' he boasted of Sam, 'I'da shit ma self... drunken Glaswegian leanin' inta ma sentry box... brave as a lion.'

Back in the marquee the Wednesday evening conversation had turned to football. Wednesday evening, Lionel figured, was philosophy evening; most men had run out of money the day before pay day and so the only thing left to do was lounge about and try and cadge a fag off someone who had some.

'How's Benny going to play football, he can't just join a team, can he?' Sid was as mystified as were the others who had little interest in the island game.

'Wh'ay man, he can,' Jackie Bones sat with a football coupon on the bed beside him. 'There's a guy runs a squad of hopefuls, he sorts the good from the bad when they get here. You cannae just join in, you have to go through him first, they have some cracking games, all sorts mixed together, some near professional and others fucking hopeless. You should come and watch one on Sunday. Me 'n' Chick and Andy always go.' The

Andy he referred to was Andy Kyle, another Glaswegian who had arrive by furniture van at Erlstoke in full Teddy boy outfit. An infectious, squeaky laugh was his tradmark.

'What is the attraction with football?'

'Wash your mouth out Sam Smart. It is a beautiful game. Just enough rules to make it fair, just enough leeway to make it tough and just enough luck to make it exciting: a perfect game.' Jackie took on a mystical look.

'What about cricket?' Sam persisted.

'Too many rules and you can't play it in the winter when the light's bad.'

'Why not?' Yorkie Carr chipped in.

'Ball's too small. Too small and too fast...'

'You could play it with a bigger ball...' The conversationalists all saw Yorkies' vision and laughed...'fucking big ball and a wide bat, just like the kids play on the beach!'

'See what I mean,' Jackie caught the conversation again, 'the whole thing becomes a farce. Football avoids all that sort of thing. Good sized pitch, enough time to get knackered but not hanging around all day. Non contact apart from accidents...'

'Fouls is what you mean,' Sid said that at school he was always encouraged to go for the man.

'That's because your such a big bugger. You should have been in a basket ball team in any case,' Jackie turned to Sam again, 'you could be a bit short for the game, couple or three inches would have you able to take a ball on your head and nod it in easily.'

Sam tried to imagine himself in football kit on some muddy field 'nodding it in'. The wet leather ball from the convent had nearly knocked him out. He listened as the conversation followed it's meandering path. Such a public conversation was the thing of barrack room life. Mostly you could hear all the conversations going on. People would dart from one to another while they sat on their bed bulling their boots. It seemed strange to him now but most barrack rooms had been cosy. A warm fug of men and cigarettes. Wafts of aftershave lotion as evening outings were dressed for: grey flannel trousers, blue blazer, Royal Engineers badge on the breast pocket.

During the first months of his service, in Gibraltar barracks, he had looked forward to the ten thirty lights out. Someone had a radio and on Sunday nights radio Luxembourg would broadcast pop music. Theresa Brewer would sing 'Put another nickel in the nickelodeon' and the voice would drift into the soft, thick darkness of the room sending him into a warm, dreamless sleep.

At other times they would sit round the stove and tell stories. Waries they became known, as tales of friends and relations who had served in the war began to be related.

'Stick your foot in a bucket of sand, swing the lights and tell us a warie.'

A game developed when it was discovered that one lad, Westy, would always go one better than any story told. If he went to the lavatory they would concoct some tale about being on the edge of a cliff and then slip it into the conversation later on. Total lies but Westy would trump it with being on a higher cliff. The hot stove, no money and nothing to do except talk and listen.

The tropical air and flapping canvas came alive once more.

'You figured out how to beat the football pools yet?' the question directed at Jackie who lifted the coupon from the bed. 'I'm workin on it man...'

'You need a radio, shortwave,' Yorkie shifted his glasses up his nose and stared blankly at the canvas wall, as if trying to work out how to use a shortwave radio to overcome the international date line. The tent fell quiet.

The Match

The pitch was fairly flat, a slight rise in one corner seemed to be used to advantage during corner kicks or throw ins as far as Sam could make any sense of it. They had gathered on the Sunday morning to watch Benny make his debut as a footballer. Mickey Doyle pretended to commentate, noting that the weather 'was dry and the playing surface firm'. The fact that the entire pitch was of dried coral mud rolled solid, hard as concrete and that it had only rained once in Sam's time on the island seemed to make the pitch report a bit superfluous.

'There aren't very many players. I always remember more,' Robbie started counting.

'Seven a side,' Jackie Bones informed him. 'This is just to see how good they are or not. The pitch is a bit undersized as well but it's the best we've got.'

A tall thin squaddie in a black shirt and shorts marched to the middle of the field, whistle in his mouth, ball crooked in his arm. He found the centre spot, a scratched circle in the clay.

'Where's the lines?' Sam wondered

'Ref knows where the lines are, and the linesmen,' Jackie pointed out the two lads who paced back and forth at the edges of the pitch. 'The important thing on this pitch is how they handle the ball. If the ball goes between the sand bags that's a goal as far as lofty's concerned. Winning or losing is not it at this stage.

'Playing the game!' Robbie put on his posh voice.

They watched as the coin was tossed, the ball placed then a toot on the whistle and the game began.

To Sam's eyes this was usually where the subtleties of the game went over his head. The ball would be passed in what seemed to him a random fashion, kicked from one running man to the next while other players skipped about, obviously a plan was being carried out. At school no such plan had emerged. All the players chased the ball, all over the field, a great heaving mass of bobbing heads and flailing arms, like an unruly flock of starlings or maybe seagulls chasing thrown bread at the seaside.

Suddenly Benny had the ball. He juggled it expertly between his flying feet, his arms wind-milling, his face a grin of pure pleasure. No one could get near, the arms and legs whirled too fast, it would have been like tackling some flailing machine. Benny scored running on between the sandbags in triumph.

The ball was retrieved. The tall referee whispered close to Benny's ear. The entire choreography started again, once more the flailing Benny ran the length of the field and scored a goal. The farce continued in a haphazard fashion until the ref finally banished the big Fijian from the field and a more ordinary game began to unfold. As boring as ever in Sam's opinion.

They quizzed Benny. What had the ref kept whispering?

'Non contact sport he say. Each time, non contact. I don't get it. I never contact nobody, just play the ball and score the goal.'

Jackie Bones took him to one side and Sam watched as Benny listened and nodded. Finally he must have got the message as he dropped his head into his hands in apparent despair.

'What did you tell him that upset him so much?' Sam asked later.

'I explained the finer points of the game,'

'The non contact bit?'

'Yeah, that and the concept of putting the ball in your opponents net.'

'No?'

'Yep. Four own goals.'

Chapter 018

Boredom

It seemed to Sam that everything was 'slipping into a slump'. He had never been that excited about being on the island, in fact very little about the army in general had ever caused any quickening of the pulse in Sam's book. It was almost a matter of principle.

To say that the days dragged by would, he thought, be wrong. Working with Robbie - they continued to clip endless miles of wire onto endless walls and beams - was easy and pleasurable in that they were largely left to their own devices. No. The days didn't drag but they had a terrible sameness. Each morning he faced this awful inevitability. The work stretched ahead. No one had any idea how many huts would make up the finished camp. The same jokes and rumours passed among the men. Yorkie Carr had injured himself while working on the roof trusses. He had, so the story went, lost his grip and caught his foot in the crook of the truss. Instead of yelling for help, so the story continued, he had hung quietly upside down while a bevy of airhostesses had passed along the road below accompanied by the usual escort of captains and lieutenants.

Sam had seen Yorkie later that week but couldn't detect any injured leg.

The cinema was a Godsend with a new film each week. The evening still good value for money at one and six. Geordie Thompson and Yorkie paid a shilling and sat right at the front, reckoned it was poor eyesight.

On one particular visit things had taken a different turn with the second reel refusing to thread into the projector. The screen had gone blank and a howl gone up from the audience.

'There will be an intermission,' came the announcement.

'How long?' went up the shout.

'Until I can get this bloody film threaded,' came the exasperated reply.

A silence followed. The stars twinkled overhead and the blank screen stared at the audience who stared back like sailors watching a sail, waiting for it to fill.

'Bones' granny swigs the meth!' A lone cry from the darkness.

'Fuck off! a broad Geordie accent indicated that Jacky Bones was in the audience.

'She sips it from a glass with a cherry on a stick in it!' The vision of the purple drink must have entered everyone's mind. A cheer went up.

'Too right,'

'My granny can't afford meths,' a new voice taking the conversation on.

'Tell her to try white spirit!'

'She uses that on her wooden leg!'

'Never mind, Sunderland'll win the cup next year...' Sam felt he must have missed something about wooden legs and football teams.

'She play for them?'

'Be a sight better than some in that team, even with a wooden leg!'

Hoots and cheers and then, suddenly the screen came alive with Gregory Peck squinting into the sun.

Jazz

'Brallient, it'll be brallient.' Louis Patchittie's Scottish accent did strange things to words.

They sat in an outdoor marquee, that was one without walls. Handy if you needed shade and, oddly enough, privacy. If you played music in a tent all the world would pop their heads in. Because you could stand back watch and listen meant that most people kept their distance; privacy in full view. Louis had dragged Sam and his guitar over to meet Pete Jones. Pete played banjo. He was ginger haired with a oval, benign looking face. An easy grin hovered about his lips constantly. He didn't say much but you could see him listening, his blue eyes following the conversation while his fingers played silent tunes on the banjo strings.

'You'll love busking,' Louis checked his tuning with Pete.

'Yeh, but it does involve playing the guitar with a certain amount of skill,' Sam said lamely. He was not sure how he would get out of this situation without offending Louis who had so far taught him all he knew. Well enough to play most of Peggy Sue.

'Listen,' Louis rested his arm across the guitar, 'with busking it's a matter of getting the audience started. Once they get the rhythm of the thing, they know the tune and off you go. It'll be Christmas, the officers mess said they would like a bit of music to help the whiskey go down...'

'Whiskey?'

'Aye, the officers have spirits. Anyway by the time we get there we will know all the tunes we need.'

'But...'

'No buts. You'll be playing trad jazz most of the time. Five chords at the most. A, E, B seven with an A minor and an E seven thrown in...' He lifted his guitar and sang the first verse of Sporting Life. Pete picked at the banjo strings adding a certain casualness to the tune as befits most jazz.

'So you play...' he nodded Sam in. The verse progressed, Louis sang and signalled the changes, Sam missed a few beats but by the time they had sung the verse five times he had the sequence pretty well off by heart.

'What happens if I get lost?'

'You won't get lost but...' Louis thought for a moment.

'Play the bottom string quietly.' Pete smiled.

and plucked the bottom string of his banjo.

The evening wore on. Louis and Pete played some really clever stuff, relegating Sam to the rank of drummer.

CHAPTER 18

Christmas time

Letter

      The letter came next. This end of year time meant nothing on the island. Back in Britain the weather would be getting colder, most men looking forward to the big break that covered Christmas and the new year. In boys service Sam remembered sneaking out at night to steal coal from the huge pile at the back of the camp. Keeping the stove hot was a major job as the days grew shorter and the billets colder.

      Here? The sun shone same as yesterday and the day before. Here someone began playing a record on the camp radio. 'How'ja like to spend Christmas on Christmas Island' would pop up and be greeted by boos and jeers. The disc jockey would stop it with a needle scratching sound. Lionel reckoned that the sound was fake.

      'The record would be unplayable by now, he's done that so many times.'

      The mail came round and Sam had a letter. From Jean. Jean. It showed her home address so no excuse, he would have to write back.

      'Dear Sam. Terry has told me a lot about you so I had better tell you a bit about me...' he read.

      'I work in a shop, well they call it a supermarket now with lots of tills, not very exciting. I live with my Mum and Dad down in Millbrook and from our house you can see the big ships that come into Southampton docks', the letter continued and mentioned places that Terry had told him about. The Bargate, The Checkpoint... 'a coffee bar that is really smooth', she said. Sam wondered what he should write back. What did this girl look like apart from being blonde? Down at the end she asked about him. 'Tell me all about yourself, how did you get to be on a desert island you lucky thing'.

      'Dear Jean,' he wrote, 'you ask me to tell you all about me, not much to tell...' he thought for a moment, 'I'm an orphan', that sounded dramatic and he wasn't really sure it was true; he had a step mother but for all they meant to each other now that Dad was dead she might just have been a kind lady who had taken him in. 'My Mum died at the end of the war and I was put into a home in Muswell Hill in London. Then I got moved into a Catholic convent because my Dad was still in the army. He came out and married Grace, my step Mother and we lived in Tooting. I skived off school, Dad found out and put me in the army as a boy soldier. Got into trouble and was shipped out to this island.'

He looked at the writing, his whole life so far in about five or six lines. Was that really it?

'I'm learning to play the guitar,' he continued, 'Louis Patchitti is teaching me. He wants to play jazz but I prefer rock and roll, Buddy Holly's 'Peggy Sue' is coming along nicely. What do you listen to?'

The rest of the letter wandered on. He hadn't been prepared for writing into a silence, he wanted smiling eyes, he wanted to watch the face of the person, wanted to gauge the impact of his words, wanted to talk to Loretta. What the hell, he sealed it and posted it. 'Play some chords,' he thought.

'How was the letter?' Terry asked later.

'Alright. She told me about all the things you've told me. What's she like?'

'Don't know really, I haven't met her much. Dor doesn't invite friends on our dates. Blonde, ordinary, not bad looking, bit plump...'

'What, fat?'

'No! Just well covered, nice tits. Wears her hair in a bun on the top of her head. She's OK. Ask her to send a photo.'

Sam wondered. He should have asked for a photo. Next time. Different to Loretta, not a school teacher but a girl on the till. Maybe that was more his level. Had that been why Loretta had not wanted to keep in touch? Thicko Sam Smart mumbling on about Buddy Holly. Not much of a future there. He began to get angry with her. Angry with the slight girl and her straight cut blonde hair. Angry with the school teacher, too good for him by half Grace would have judged. Angry with her smiling eyes...Then he wanted her again, closed his eyes, held her close just clinging on, nothing else, just hold her. The sob welled in his throat and he struck the guitar strings hard.

'Shut up fer Christ's sake!' someone shouted.

Christmas

Christmas approached in a way that Christmas had never approached before. Obviously it didn't get cold, but that wasn't it.

'It's the height of summer at Christmas time in Australia,' Lionel told Sam when he raised the subject. 'They have Christmas dinner outside,'

'Silly sods,' Tommy Marks chipped in his bit.

'No, what I'm saying,' Lionel persisted, 'is that we think of Christmas as cold the same as the Aussies think of it as hot and a lot of what we think has been shaped by writers like Dickens who always have it snowing all the time. Most of our Christmas's are wet and gloomy.'

'So this one is going to be an Aussie Christmas,' Sam concluded, 'I'm still not eating my Christmas pud outside.'

'You wait till you get down to the officers mess on Christmas eve,' Louis Patchitti joined in, 'one of the blokes who's batting for Richardson reckons that they are going to have a big midnight feast with tables full of food and whiskey!'

'I bet they don't,' Lionel leaned forward. 'Midnight Mass more likely!'

'You reckon?' Louis looked unsure. 'I'd better check.'

It was a good job he did. Sure enough the officers mess was booked for midnight mass so Louis moved the busking to Christmas evening. Then Sam's guitar gave up the ghost. Well for a minute it became a ghost.

It lived hanging from a cord attached to the marquee brailing - Sam knew it was a brailing from Boys Brigade camp - just behind his head and within easy reach should a sudden urge to play E or any of the other five chords that Sam had learned. Sam lay on his canvas bed thinking about, well nothing really. His mind dipped into the soft conversations that would drift about, picking up a word or thought here and there, turning it over then forgetting it.

His guitar suddenly played a loud chord which was strangled almost at birth leaving just a gentle rhythmic tapping as if waiting for a voice to sing.

'What the f...' Sam sat up. There hung the guitar as it usually did but then he noticed that the bridge hung loose swaying slightly on the end of its six strings. He lifted it down gently and cradled it like an injured animal. His beloved Vos guitar. Broken.

'LOUIS!'

Move it.

Jean sent him a record request as a Christmas present. Cliff Richard's 'Move It'. The whole bunch of them in the NAAFI cheered as the announcer read out 'From Jean in Southampton to Sam on his desert island. Happy Christmas Sam.' then Cliff sang 'come on pretty baby letsa move it and groove it...'

'Phwoa! Mooove it and Groove it... she's ready for a bit of groovin' '

Sam shrunk himself into his seat and prayed for the record to stop.

Christmas eve and he had got out of midnight mass, being RC, and decided to write to Jean.

'Dear Jean,' he wrote, 'thank you for the record request. All my mates took the micky out of me while it was playing. I reckon most of the blokes on the island know who I am by now. They reckon you were being suggestive but I don't think so.'

He would see how she reacted to that. If it had been suggestive of something more this would be the key that unlocked it.

'Could you send me a photo of yourself? I don't really know what you look like so it's like writing to an imaginary person...'

An imaginary person? What the fuck was he going on about?

'I mean a person that only exists in my mind from what Terry has told me...' That was little better but it would have to do.

'My guitar broke, the bridge came unstuck from the front. Louis got the chippy to fix it so now it is stronger than ever but it doesn't quite ring as much, the sound is a bit dead. Still, with my playing that is probably a good thing. Tomorrow night I have to go busking in the officers mess. Louis' idea. Me, him and Pete Jones on banjo. God knows what it will sound like. Louis reckons they will all be p,' he crossed the p out, 'drunk so it won't matter.'

'By the time you get this Christmas will be over and it will be heading for the time when I come home. Then we will meet.'

Well obviously they would meet. Prat. The thought stayed. They had turned the corner, January February March. Say it quick and not long, say it in weeks, ten, say it in days seventy odd. The thought cheered him up.

'Ten weeks or so; not long.'

Christmas day

Christmas day dawned.

'It should be snowing and me Mam should be in the kitchen cursing a turkey that was too big fer the oven. Dad having the first fag of the day and inspecting his shave in one of the glass balls on our Christmas tree. Instead of which we get excused reveille!' Scouse finished his speech and lit a cigarette.

'Lucky bugger with a turkey,' Tommy Marks lit his own cigarette, 'we had to make do with a chicken.'

'We had a duck once,' Yorkie Carr fitted his glasses arms round his ears and pushed the bridge up into its groove.

'That's all out for nothing ain't it?' Tommy wondered.

'Better than chicken,' Yorkie retaliated. 'nice dark meat, very tasty.

'D'you have and quackers with it?' Sid with a rare one liner. A communal groan went round the tent.

The day began as a Sunday would have started. Some woke, some remained asleep oblivious of the sparkling conversation that twinkled around them. Sam reached up and touched his wounded guitar. First public appearance tonight. Maybe he should tell Louis he was sick. Sick on Christmas day!

Bollocks! That would mean the he would miss a pretty good breakfast and at lunch time a Christmas dinner. All of the Christmas dinners he had had in the army had been on the last day before Christmas eve when most of the camp had been ready to shove off home. Beer on the table and the officers doing the waiting. Bringing the plates of food to the table rather than the usual self service. This Christmas dinner on Christmas day; fitting, as they were on Christmas Island. Sam wondered how many times he had said the word!

He remembered a last night before Christmas leave in Chatham. Two Christmas's ago and still doing his trade training. All down to the Golden Lion in Brompton High Street: The Beast as it was known. Scrumpy was the drink, rough cider Sam was told, being made of apples it was good for you. A shot of blackcurrant took the bitterness off.

'Two pints of Diesel and a shot of Redex, la,' Scouse ordered using the nickname the engine fitters used for the drink.

'Gerit down you,' Scouse slide the pint over to Sam and the pair drank quietly for a moment. 'Ey, Tottie.' The Liverpudlean nudged Sam.

'That's Janet and her mate. Jan!' Sam called them over, 'come and meet Scouse, funniest man in Chatham.'

'Nice way to introduce a man,' Scouse protested

'Hello Scouse,' the girls spoke together.

'I'm Pat,' the dark girl introduced herself. She moved closer to the Liverpudlean. 'Why Scouse? she asked.

'I'm from Liverpool, it's what we eat up there; stew, meat and spuds, carrots and onions and, if you're lucky, a splash of Worcester sauce, the only foreign thing me Mam would allow.' He closed his eyes and remembered the taste. 'If times were hard you could have blind scouse...'

'What was that?' Pat was smiling her 'like you' smile.

'Leave the meat out. Or you could have totally disabled scouse.

'Which was?' Pat smiled the smile again.

'Soup!'

'Tell them what you call bubble and squeak, cold spuds and cabbage from the Sunday menu, fried up on Monday.'

'Oh, aiy; resurrection!'

'Brilliant name. Get you a drink ladies?' Sam felt generous with his leave pay in his pocket. In boys service it had been a white fiver, something you saw only once a year.

That evening had been memorable. The cold Chatham evening held at bay by the drink. He remembered snow on the ground as he had made love to Jan against a wall in a dark back alley. A knee trembler with the danger that she might lose her footing on the trampled snow! They had moved on to The Sawyers, a pub across the road if you didn't take the detour through the alley. Sam remembered they had 'gone along the top shelf' a ritual of drinking a tot of each liqueur. Sam's last memory had been Tia Maria. The sweet coffee flavour still lingered in his memory, associated with lots of spewing and the worst hangover ever the next morning. Briefly during the night he had remembered a cat on his bed.

'Funniest thing ever,' Robbie remembered, 'Sam pissed out of his head trying to stroke this cat he called Timmy. Nobody else could see it but it must have jumped off the bed. Sam went after it and collapsed. We stuck a pillow under his head and a couple of blankets over him and he stayed quiet all night.

The next morning they had gone on a route march.

'Five miler, nothing strenuous, just get the blood pumping a bit.' The corporals called out the pace and they marched off around the nearest bit of countryside. A good natured route march with all the usual jokes and the left foot stamp every eight paces. The corporals allowed them the fun. Normally they shouted for silence.

Back and then the Christmas lunch. Sam felt slightly better and Robbie poured him a brown ale.

'Hair of the dog,' he grinned, 'or cat! Timmy Timmy Timmy!'

'What the fuck are you on about mate?'

'Nothing,' Robbie grinned the more.

The tables were laid out with bottled beer and holly decorations and the officers had begun their waiting duties...

That evening had gone a long way to curbing Sam's drinking. He remembered Jan his seductress but the subsequent boozing and spewing had knocked most of the pleasurable memory from his mind.

As for Scouse, he seemed able to drink forever without getting more than slightly tipsy.

Coming back from that Christmas leave they had arrived on the same train. Once in barracks Sam had unpacked a bottle of aftershave, a present from step mother Grace.

'What do you think of that?' he said handing it to Scouse for a sniff.

Scouse took it, unscrewed the cap and took a copious swig!

'Not bad, bit sweet but ok.'

Sam smiled and touched his guitar again. Busking tonight.

Breakfast

'Breccy,' Yorkie Carr hauled his shorts and jacket on.
'Good idea,' Sam was starving.
'Bring us back a mug of tea...' Tommy reached for his mug.
'Piss off, it's Christmas day,' said Yorkie feeling that was excuse enough.

They walked over to the cookhouse.

The vast marquee had been decorated ready for the lunch.

'Where did they get all this crepe paper and tinsel?' Sam wondered.

'It's Christmas Island,' Yorkie grinned making his glasses sparkle on his nose, 'grows on trees this time of the year.' he pushed the glasses up into place.

The army tried its best, Sam thought, someone somewhere had ordered a consignment of Christmas decorations to be shipped halfway round the world so that squaddies like him and Yorkie could feel a bit more cheerful at breakfast. He began to realise that he questioned very little of what happened behind the scenes. He took large parts of his experience at face value. Like a stone age man staring out at the universe, he took it all for granted. Another thought followed on: the stone age man had eventually begun to wonder, to question.

The mood was jolly and the bacon seemed somehow sizzlier. Breakfast had started later so perhaps this explained it.

'What we doing today then?'

'Good question. Bugger all I reckon.' Sam was good at doing bugger all.

They both filled their mugs and walked back to the marquee.

'You can have half,' he told Tommy, decanting the sweet tea into Tommy's waiting mug.

NAAFI break arrived. Those who had missed breakfast now bought tomatoes on toast and Cornish pasties. Sam had a pastie with plenty of Del Monte ketchup. The air was filled with the smell of toast, coffee, cigarette smoke and last night's beer. Camp radio had started with 'Howdya like to spend Christmas... The announcer had skidded the needle and then a crack signalled that he had broken the record.

'Five pieces!' he yelled, 'they will be framed for all to see!'

A great cheer filled the vast, hangar like building.

'A head on a pole to prove it,' Lionel said.

Lunch

The cookhouse had been extended to accommodate all the inhabitants of Main Camp, tables pushed into long lines.

'Like the beer fests in Germany,' Robbie had been. He poured brown ale from the bottle. 'We'll all be linking arms and singing umpapa music. Cheers.'

The ritual began again. The officers began to bring the plates piled high with turkey and roast potatoes, sprouts and carrots, stuffing, little sausages and...

'Jam!' Sam pointed his knife at the red mound.

'Cranberry sauce you peasant. Sets the turkey off a treat.' Robbie was tucking in. Sam tried it. Liked it and remembered eating peaches and ham with Loretta high on Diamond head. What would she be doing now? Did they celebrate Christmas in America? Sure they did, he'd seen a film with Bing Crosby about Christmas. What was Thanksgiving then? If only he could go to Washington and find her. The sob threatened to overwhelm the turkey.

The commanding officer took the stage and silence fell.

'Men' Sam guessed this wasn't aimed at the two WVS ladies who hovered about the tables.

'Men, this has been a momentous year. Great Britain now stands shoulder to shoulder with America ready to protect civilisation against threat.' he paused. 'The devices that we have seen tested have been found true, these devices will ensure peace for centuries to come, their very presence a deterrent to any invader. A ban on further tests has been called for so that our enemies cannot benefit from similar weapons. It is with this in mind that I wish you all a very merry Christmas and a Happy New year. Peace on earth. The Queen.'

Mugs were raised and the shout went up. 'The Queen!'

Thoughts of home

Their bellies full, the gathering came slowly to a close. Sam and the others wandered back to the tents. The sun was high and hot, 'very un Christmas like,' Sam thought.

The fact that there may be no more tests opened the possibility of a shortened tour.

'Send us all home I reckon,' Tommy flopped onto his bed and joined his hands over his full stomach. The struts pinged their protest.

'Not before we've finished,' the cold water of Lionel's reasoning cast a shadow over the return home theory.

'Finished what?' Yorkie Carr fiddled with something from his bedside box.

'The camp,' Lionel sat up, 'We've got all this kit out here, huts half finished, sewage system in place, you don't think they're going to let all that go to waste? No I think we'll finish our full tour.'

'What d'you reckon it'll be used for?' Tommy wondered lazily.

'A long runway in the middle of the Pacific with a sea port for really heavy equipment. Accommodation for thousands of personnel, half way between America and China by the back door! Use your noddle.' Lionel lay back on his bed to think about these things. Strategic planning. He liked the idea.

    Sam also lay thinking. He thought about Christmas day back home. Dad had married into a large family. As far as Sam could remember Dad's Scottish family was a faint memory from childhood. Auntie Peg in Montrose, Auntie Carrie in Stirling. He had no idea if they were real or honourary aunties. Why didn't he know all this?

    The Wiltshire side of Mum's family was just Auntie Jean and he hadn't seen her since his convent days. So he had no grand-mothers, no grand-fathers. He grew to be more and more an orphan as the days passed.

    Grace was a different matter. The Buttles were cockneys and it seemed that they had taken Dad to their hearts. They told the story of his first appearance at their table. When asked if he wanted more he replied that he had had 'an elegant sufficiency, thank you.'

    'Very Clarke's College,' they all said, then smiled affectionately.

    He remembered one particular Christmas at Elsie's. That Christmas morning had been sunny. Mum and Sam had walked from home, up the length of Southcroft Road; wide and open Southcroft road more spacious than Gassiot Road, bungalows at intervals, front gardens pushing the houses away from the pavement. Up the steps to the front door. Fred lets them in. Henry is already there, big in his three piece suit, his waist coat rounding out from the jacket, well fed, his blond hair waved - always a joke with Bill who was almost bald; 'his hair waved, waved goodbye!' Fred serving sherry. Fred with his dark hair slicked back, his pipe clenched firmly between his teeth. Fred quiet and kind.

    Sam remembered him mending shoes in his shed. Fred made shoes for cripples and loved his job. At the week end he would repair all the family's shoes. Hammer away in his shed while Sam beat nails flat and made spears to be thrown at the back fence. Rexy, Fred's dog, would move among the gathering, his tail always at a slow wag, his patient kindness the same as his master's, he let himself be stroked then moved on to be stroked again. He had only ever snapped at Sam once when, much younger, Sam had knelt down beside his bowl just he was about to eat. 'Thinks your going to steal it,' Fred had said, his pipe wagging between his clenched teeth.

    That Christmas in front of the fire in the front room at Southcroft road filled his dreaming mind now. A comic annual from Elsie and Fred. Lots to read but for the moment held by a big illustration. A man eating caterpillar emerging from a fire filled cave on the side of a volcano. The picture captivated Sam. The fire in the grate became the cave and Sam peered into the depths between the coals.

    Lunch at the long table, chicken? Perhaps turkey, he couldn't remember. A long afternoon, much like the one on the island as he lay half asleep. The adults talked, Sam read his annual.

    Tea and then the radiogram. Elsie had all the latest things. In 1952 they had all watched the coronation on a nine inch screen television set, the small black and white picture a marvel in Elsie's back room. Grace said that Els' and Fred ate all their meals in front of the television, trays perched on their laps. Sam felt that Grace didn't quite approve. The radiogram was better. Billy Cotton's band show would entertain them on Sundays. Long playing records would provide music for Henry to sing to. He sang well, a rich tenor. He would dab his forehead in the manner of the operatic singers who sweated on the stages of the world's opera houses.

    Bill sang. London songs with catchy rhythms that hitched the legs of dancing women. 'Abe, Abe, Abe my boy, vot are you vaiting for now?' he would add the Jewish vees and persuade Sam up onto the imaginary stage to learn and sing at the same time moving his feet in the lazy cockney shuffle that the music hall comedians adopted. He would be busking tonight, he was not sure if he could move his feet and get a b seven chord at the same time. Sam stared at the gently flapping tent roof and reached up to touch his guitar.

Was that family? They were warm hearted people, welcoming Dad and himself into their midst. Friday nights would see them gathered at the family home in Smallwood road Tooting. Friday night was cards night. Grace had made little money bags which they filled with pennies and half pennies so that they could gamble. They played Whist or Newmarket or Sevens. Sam joined in sometimes but never had the brain for cards. Dad would make them all laugh and Grace would spend a deal of time saying 'Alan!' as he came out with something a bit near the knuckle.

Ciss, the oldest of the daughters, was big, blonde and florid. Doll, the youngest had dark straight hair and tended an allotment. Ciss sat in the chair that was most difficult to move from, she therefore controlled the proceedings and had everything brought to her. Reg had been a soldier. He was thin and upright with a soldier's humour. 'Aldershit' he had informed Sam prior to boys service. He never told stories of his army service. This thought almost roused Sam from his Christmas afternoon reverie in the middle of the Pacific. Not once.

Bert smoked and so his fingers were brown as stained wood. These fingers drummed; intricate rhythms tapped out while the cards were dealt. The small room yellow and warm, the iron range crackled and shifted in its alcove. Cigarettes were lit, silent concentration furrowed brows, coins chinked from bags and were stacked like casino chips on the oilcloth table cover. Bets were made, the kitty added to. Sam felt he was a guest. Family they were but in Sam's mind him and Dad were outsiders, not a real family in their own home; real mum Cath, Dad and John.

The lunch had been good. Sam fell asleep as if some conclusion had been reached.

Busking

The officers mess was very different. Fairy lights had been rigged and long tables, filled with plates of food, had been laid out. The officers stood around drinking and laughing, taking food from the tables, smoking. Louis, Pete Jones and Sam joined this throng almost unnoticed. Carrying their instruments they sought out lieutenant Richards.

'Lads, welcome to the officers paradise,' lieutenant Richards swayed toward them a broad grin on his face. 'My minstrels indeed.' Louis asked about what was expected.

'The floor is yours,' young officer made a gesture spilling some wine in the process.

'Can we eat any of the buffet?' Pete asked.

'Of course you can, can't have you playing on an empty stomach can we. Listen,' he gathered them close becoming conspiratorial, 'would you like some whisky? Haven't had a dram in a wee while eh!' his Scottish accent caused Louis to wince.

'That would be lovely,' Pete chipped in again, anxious to keep the conversation on track.

'Good, help yourselves to some nibbles and I will be right back with the drinkees,' he touched his nose and weaved off to the bar.

They tuned. Sam quaked.

'Rock Island Line...' Louis nodded and Pete played the chuntering arpeggio on the banjo. Louis roared the opening lines, Sam strummed, sweated but then realised the that the audience had gathered in front of them, clapping out the rhythm and singing along with Louis' gruff Scottish voice.

As Louis had said, once they got the tune you just kept the beat going and everybody was happy. Louis would shout the chord changes when Sam stumbled and no one seemed to notice. Lieutenant Richards brought them a tray of drinks, beers round the outside still in the can and three triple whiskies crowded into the middle away from prying eyes. They ate, drank, played. Watched officers dancing with officers, lifting their legs to the jazzy tunes.

Pete did a solo that had more notes in it that seemed possible. Cheers went up as his fingers flew against the strings. Sweat glistened on his brow. Sam felt better than he had felt for a long time. He vowed he would keep on with the guitar, vowed that one day he would hold an audience, make it whoop and cheer, dance and clap. With rock and roll girls might even swoon. He drained the forbidden whisky glass.

At twelve Christmas day ended. Lieutenant Richards, still upright but leaning a little more, approached.

'No last waltz, wouldn't be appropriate there being no ladies to waltz with. Thank you lads, you've livened up the proceedings no end.' He weaved off raising his glass high and looking back at them.

'Right, that's us then,' Louis wiped the frets of his guitar, 'let's make a quick getaway, I'm gonna have that pineapple.'

The fruit still graced the centre of the table. Sam helped himself to a couple of sausage rolls and Pete filled his pockets with some wall nuts. Louis grasped the pineapple's prickly crest and the three marched off into the night Louis not noticing that all he had was the crest. The fruit had been sliced ready for eating.

CHAPTER 20

The end of the year

New Year's Eve

'London really pisses me off!'

New Year's eve saw the NAAFI packed for the evening. Sam and Sid had grabbed a long bench, not the best seat but comfortable enough to down a few beers. Then the stranger came and sat on the end, Geordie's place.

'Someone's seat, mate.' Sam had said and the stranger gave his opinion about London.

'Why's that? Sam had asked. He should have known better, the bloke was obviously pissed.

'Cos I say so,' he jerked a cigarette from his tin, found his lighter and aimed the flame at the end managing to burn the fag half way along it's length in the process. 'savin' seats, that's fucking Londoners, always think they're better...'

'No, it's just my mate's seat.' Sam's London accent seemed to incense the drunk more.

'Cunt!' the stranger drew his fist back, Sam ducked and felt the blow pass his ear. He dived forward and turned to find the stranger on the floor, his cigarette broken and his can glugging beer onto the concrete.

'Fucking hell! How'd he get there?'

'I figured he needed hitting so I hit him,' Sid retrieved his can from the table, 'good job you ducked.'

Geordie came back and sat on the end of the bench, the drunk staggered off swearing.

'You been fighting?'

'No, just saving your seat...'

'Look,' Sid interrupted the conversation and pointed to the far corner of the vast shed, 'where'd that come from?'

A vast tower of cans loomed almost to the ceiling, the latest Tower of Piss up! Taller than anything they had seen before.

'I never noticed them building that,' Sid stood up for a better view.

'Too busy fighting,' Geordie reckoned.

'Something not right,' said Sam, 'they would have been attacked, cans flying, long before they got half way that high.' Sam had seen it happen so many times before. Almost on cue the first can was thrown hitting the tower half way up. It bounced off! A roar went up and more cans were thrown, they all bounced off. The tower remained standing. Then it dawned.

'The crafty sods have welded it,' Geordie gave a whoop, 'reckon they smuggled it in sideways.'

Nineteen fifty eight came to a noisy close. Songs were sung, arms linked for auld lang syne with pulling and pushing getting rowdier, people falling over. Someone let off a banger. Sam wondered where you would get a banger in the middle of the Pacific? He wondered if it was the New Year in Tooting. Grace didn't go in for that sort of thing. Dad would have, being from Aberdeen. He would have known what Auld Lang syne meant.

What a year fifty eight had been, starting off with the nick and ending up being almost punched by a London hating drunk. Loretta marked the midpoint. He felt the sob even now standing in this riot of sound, saw her smile, saw her brimming eyes as the lift door closed between them on that awful Sunday night.

Geordie thrust another can into his hand.

'Whey aye man, drink up. The new year's here, nineteen fifty fucking nine. Soon be March and time to go home. I'm gonna shag my self witless all my disembark leave.'

'January, February, March,' Sam counted, 'then home, back to Gassiot Road and step mother Grace. Maybe a months' leave. No girlfriends... well a possibility in Trowbridge or maybe the pen friend or buy himself out and go to Washington? Build a space ship and fly to the moon, that would be easier.'

The 'tower of piss up' crashed down among the tables.

Jean

The marquees began to come down and they moved into the fresh built huts. Lights, plugs, bogs that flushed with doors that let men masturbate in peace. Windows that opened like Venetian blinds, slats of glass rather than panes and at night silence. No tap tap tap of canvas in the constant trade wind.

'And the guitar sounds a whole lot better,' Louis Patchitti loved it. 'The canvas used to soak up the sound.'

Jim Heywood sat playing Sam's guitar, as usual. Yorkie Carr wrinkled his glasses further up his nose. Robbie smoked and listened. Sam opened his letter.

'Dear Sam,

Thank you for your letter. So exciting to get Air Mail letters. Christmas Island does sound fun, sailing across a lagoon is something I only see at the pictures.
Not much seems to happen in Southampton. Now that Terry is away Doreen doesn't like to go out too much and so life gets a bit dull for all of us. Christmas and the New Year were much the same as always.

The big towers made of beer cans sound frightening. What if one fell on you? You said they were welded together so they would be pretty solid, give you quite a whack.

Fancy you being good enough at the guitar to play at the officer's mess. I would have been terrified. I never was much good at music, just about managed a simple tune on the recorder at school. That wouldn't have been much use. I prefer listening to it. Hope you enjoyed my record request for you. Bet all your mates laughed.

Not long until March. Will you be coming down to Southampton to see me when you get home? That would be nice.'

The letter continued, chit chat about this and that. Would he go and see her?

'Where's Southampton,' he asked Terry Ogilvy who still occupied the next space to him in the huts.

'England, middle of the south coast. Can't miss it.'

'What, near Brighton?' Sam's memory of geography only included Canada and Egypt.

'No, near the isle of Wight.'

'Been there, we went on Boys Brigade camp, can't remember seeing Southampton though. Portsmouth we went from.'

Camp

The train from London took them all down to Portsmouth; the ninetieth London Company Boys Brigade. Excited, noisy and filled with wonder as they arrived at the station and filed onto the big paddle steamer for the crossing to the Isle of Wight. The thump of paddles as the boat moved away was like a heartbeat. They leaned over the side to watch the furious mashing then explored to find the engine room with the vast cranks turning in the confined space and the long, silver gleaming piston rods pushing, pushing, pushing. The summer air was cool as they crossed the Solent. The brass figures on their pill box hats glinting in bright seaside sunshine.

Another train from the ferry, down the long pier with the sea beneath the sleepers and then, finally, a coach up to the camp. They were on the top of Culver cliff, the English channel on three sides.

That arrival had been a bit like the Christmas Island arrival, thought Sam. Same procedure; troops arriving at a new location. They had been assigned tents. Round tents, first world war tents, eight man tents even though they were only boys. Next an issue of palliasses, great hessian bags that were rushed over to a barn to be filled with hay. Stuffing the sacks a noisy, dusty, sneeze making operation. Captain Freeman showing how it should be done. Some boys, having stuffed too much into the sack that it now resembled a giant sausage, pulling handfuls out.

That had been the first real outing that Sam had experienced. Far from home he wondered if Dad and Grace missed him as he laid out his palliass and lay back looking at the top of the tent. The seams going up, darker than the white panels, and gathering at the top of the pole. He had remembered the convent and the first day in that quiet room, watching the flies buzz against the ceiling.

He wondered if he should tell Jean about his boys brigade camp. Maybe not.

Was there a boat from Southampton to the island? What would he tell her? Bloody cold, he remembered. Brailing. The word popped into his mind.

Each morning they were awakened with a trumpeted reveille. Wash and then sort the crumpled bedding out and roll the brailing up neatly. The wind from the sea, morning fresh and cold. Short trousers and tent inspection. Apart from the temperature it could have been a rehearsal for the Christmas Island. Wight island, a taste of what is to come. Not just a week or two but twelve bloody months. Only the brailing was different. In the round tents is was the wall that came from the sloping roof to the ground, maybe eighteen inches high and in sections to match the roof. Brailing; a nice word. Something busy about it. You could brail, be brailing.

There had been a Sunday church parade during their stay. The band had gathered at the head of the column. Sam in the third row with a trumpet which he did not play. He mimed playing as they marched to the church then mimed all the way around various locations. He just made up the ranks. When he joined the Boys Brigade he had wanted to play a drum but it turned out that everyone wanted to play a drum. All that flash stuff with the sticks, holding them up to your mouth then lefting and righting fit to bust. And doing drum rolls. Very glamorous the drum. He had been handed a trumpet - longer than a bugle - and encouraged to play. He remembered that no one had taken any time to teach him and assumed that it must be a skill that just came, or not depending on if you could or couldn't. He could only ever summon single notes from the thing with no hint of a tune.

One evening he had come home from BB and sat himself in front of the fire putting his trumpet down by his chair. Dad sat at the opposite side of the fire reading the evening paper. Suddenly the trumpet sounded a note. 'Parp!'. They both stared at the instrument.

'My trumpet played! Did you hear it Dad? It played a note.

'Have you been blowing it a lot this evening?' Dad folded his paper and leaned over to examine the instrument.

'Parp!' the trumpet sounded again. Dad started back his eyebrows raised in surprise.

'Been blowing it a lot and some notes still trapped inside, that'll be what it is.'

The trumpet had continued to sound and it was not until Sam put it on the table that he realised the sound was coming from the grate. Dad had found that pushing his leather slipper against the brass fire surround made just the right sound; the sound of a trumpet. Dad grinned and refilled his pipe. Grace brought a cup of tea in for them both and Sam gave up his fire side chair for her. They tried the trick on her but she soon discovered the cause.

'Smart woman, Grace Smart'. Dad loved playing with words.

Nothing that he could put in a letter to a girl.

Boys Brigade had punctuated his week; band practice - just marching for Sam - on Tuesday evenings then gymnastics on

Friday. A reluctant gymnast he had, however, been the top of the pyramid in the gym. Being small by comparison with most of the boys he was the light weight lad that climbed the swaying bodies to finally take his place at the top, his feet firmly on the shoulders of the two boys below, their hands holding his calves. He would fling his hands high and wait for the shout or the applause. Then the long jump down and a forward roll. Head stands, hand stands, cartwheels and back flips, all added to the general torment of Friday evenings. He could still do head stands but had never mastered the hand stand and the back flip was always beyond his abilities. He remembered that they called the evening a 'drill' evening. Mac had been in charge, a wiry Scotsman with black wavy hair. He was kind and patient. Sam supposed he would have to be kind, if a kid didn't like it he wouldn't go and the class would diminish.

The brothers Davis were the backbone of the evening, two big lads; the base of the pyramid. He remembered that he didn't much enjoy the two hours. The evening always finished with a game of handball each of the Davis lads choosing their team. If there was an uneven number Sam usually managed to fill the part of spectator. Dark evenings, evenings that made him fitter and, he supposed, evenings that had helped prepare him for army life.

Sam folded the letter and put it away in his locker.

'How's your fingers?' he took the guitar from Jim who lit a ciggy for them both.

CHAPTER 21

Heel kicking

Days to do.

Sam's days to do chart began to look meaningfully optimistic. Three months from new year.

'Ninety days,' drawled Scouse, 'like they do in the States; send him down for ninety days...'

Well it was less than ninety days, that was for sure. Nobody knew the precise departure day but a year from twenty fifth of March last, well. The posting was for a year he hoped. Waiting for the end had the usual effect. The end seemed more distant each day. Tempers frayed in the hot huts. Dear John letters seemed to arrive in even greater numbers.

'Been waiting for nine months, not up the duff and met some other bloke...' Robbie had the thing all sewn up. 'Made sure I didn't start anything before I came to Erlestoke. Could have been a three year tour as far as I knew.'

'Wise old git, aren't you,' Geordie Thompson joined the conversation.

Robbie ignored him.

'I would have fancied that little Jill girl,' Sam remembered the little blonde who now merged with Loretta in his mind.

'You're a lucky git, get the choice of all the birds, don't ya,' Geordie looked angry.

'No,' Sam felt that luck was a bit daft, 'I never got to go out with Jill...'

'Yeh, but the girl at Hickam on the fourth of July? You could have had her if her boyfriend hadn't caught you. You got in the shit and I got you out of it and never a 'ta mate', ungrateful bugger. I should have let the big bloke eat you.'

'I was grateful but I reckon I could have talked him round...'

'Then you get another one...' Geordie interrupted. Sam wondered why he should take this sort of shit. It was all past, all done with.

'Loretta.' he said her name, resenting the fact that Geordie should think of her as another one.

'Yeh, Loretta. Waltz off with her and leave your mates to get on with it.'

'What, did you expect me to invite you lot along?' Sam felt angry.

'She could have had a mate...'

'She didn't...'

'Well you wasted that one, didn't shag her!'

Sam felt his temper rising, he stood up, pushed Geordie away and never saw the fist coming that hit him in the left ear. The noise and sudden pain collapsed him onto the bed.

Geordie stood over him 'Don't you ever push me Smart.' he turned on his heel and left the room slamming the door behind him.

'Jesus that hurts' Sam sat up. The other men in the room sat in silence.

Debbie Hollingsworth came and sat beside him.

'You poor old bugger, fancy thinking you could shove Geordie about when he's in one of his argumentative moods'.

'What's up with him?'

'Bad letter from his mate, seems someone else is going out with Annabel.'

'Who the fuck's Annabel?' Sam cupped his throbbing ear.

'Some bird he was seeing before we left, he doesn't keep in touch with her much, in fact I think he is the only one who thinks they are a couple. she's a bit of a free spirit. Come on, tea time.'

They collected their eating irons and headed off to the cookhouse. Sam's ear throbbed and he cupped it once more.

'Don't worry, only a tap in Geordie terms, it won't become a cauliflower... perhaps,' Debbie laughed. 'Good job he didn't get really mad, we'd have had to bury you at sea!'

Sam blew his nose and winced as the ear throbbed, he didn't think that was funny. What would he do next time he saw Geordie?

The Cat

'We can keep it as a pet. Plenty of grub from the cookhouse, it's a cat so you don't have to take it for a walk. It finds its own place to shit and covers it up afterwards' Johnny Keene placed the cardboard box on the end of his bed and sat back.

'D'you have to keep it in a box?' Sid asked.

'Bloke bought some cats out here a while back,' Johnny explained, ignoring Sid's question, 'they've bred and I got one off a bloke in three eight. It's only little, a kitten really. Want to see it?' Johnny had an audience. He began to undo the string then reached back for a pair of wiring gloves, the sort they had all used when dealing with barbed wire back in training.

'D'you have to wear gloves as well?' enquired Sid moving further back up his bed.

Johnny explained. 'It's only little and gets nervous when handled, the bloke told me. Nervous kittens scratch in self defence, he said, so best be on the safe side.' He pulled open the top flaps of the box and was about to open the inner flaps when they exploded upwards. The ball of fur climbed up Johnny and leapt from his head to the wall then clawed itself up to the top where it clung onto the wood silently baring its teeth at the men below.

'Fucked if I'm taking it for a walk!' said Sid.

'You don't have to,' Johnny stood up and proffered the open box in the cat's direction, 'it's a cat.'

The cat stayed with them for an hour. Yorkie Carr went to the cookhouse and got a mug of milk. Sid prodded at it with a broom. Interest waned, the milk grew warm, the door swung in the breeze and then it was gone. The same dash, the same ball of fur and claws hurtling across the floor and out. Johnny closed the box.

Sam liked Johnny, the man who could drive anything on wheels or tracks. He had gone on a driving lesson with Dad once. The hill start was the subject on that particular day. Sam sat in the back watching his Dad concentrate as he drove them to a suitable hill; a residential street that sloped down to the Thames. The practice began. The clutch - Sam had no idea what a clutch did but clutch it didn't and they began to roll back toward the river.

'Brake!' the driving instructor shouted. Dad braked. Sam wondered if they would gradually descend the hill in three yard reverses. He supposed that the only way out was to get to the bottom and then do three point turns. Eventually the clutch did it's job and they began to climb the hill. The revs and the clutch became the background of that day. Dad had learned to drive and the Ford Anglia, in Saxon Grey, had become the focus of each weekend. Long drives into the country following Auntie Elsie, she in a Ford Prefect which was superior to the Anglia. Box hill became the place to visit with roads climbing up to the beauty spot and countless places called 'Little Switzerland'. Sam had sat in the back then, bored to death with scenery that comprised nothing but green hedges. When they returned they dropped Grace off and then drove down to a lockup garage where Dad would reverse in under Sam's guidance. They would walk back home but Sam could not remember any conversation although he had no memory of his father being particularly quiet. They must have talked about something.

  That was the problem with the past, so much of it had been swamped by the present. The strange world of the army had taken over his life; a world of rules and regulations that pressed down on each moment. A hierarchy of sergeants and corporals, captains, majors all with absolute control over his life. How many times had he found himself in trouble for some minor incident.

  'Report to me, six o'clock this evening, with a brush!' The favourite words of the sergeant Kent imposing some punishment for not having his bed area tidy enough or his brasses clean. His mind constantly trying to avoid the stupefying inanity of sweeping sand from the guardroom veranda or peeling spuds with an ordinary knife. What did Dad talk about? He remembered when he had bought an air pistol. They had taken the gun with them and walked by the river. Sam had been in the army a few months and could now afford such things.

  Dad had taken the pistol and shot at a squirrel getting close enough to make the animal lose its footing.

  'Winged him,' he had laughed. Sam thought this would be a good time to bring up the subject of smoking. Once in the army everyone seemed to smoke and Sam had been no exception seeking to emulate Hussey, a stylish lad, good looking and always well turned out. Hussey smoked a cigarette in the manner of Humphrey Bogart, casually held in the crook of his index finger. Sam had purchased five Woodbines and resumed his schoolboy attempts at cigarette smoking but without choking after each inhalation.

'What would you say if I took up smoking?' he asked Dad now.

Dad's reply had been gentle enough. He had pointed out that Sam was a man now. He had suggested that if he were to take it up maybe a pipe would be more the thing as it got rid of the brown goo but that basically, as he smoked himself, he felt that he could not object.

In a classic dumb move Sam had produced his cigarette case, flipped it open with ease, offered his Dad one and then lit it, expertly, with a lighter.

Dad had smoked in silence and given Sam the air pistol back.

'Twat' Sam said the word aloud now.

'Who's a twat?' Johnny Keene asked.

'No, I was just thinking,' said Sam.

Buddy

It had come on the news, a plane crash had killed Buddy Holly and the Big Bopper. Flying out of Fargo the plane came down in a snow storm. Sam hauled his guitar down and strummed through 'Peggy Sue', surely his favourite record. He remembered the excited thrill when he had first heard the song. That had started his whole guitar adventure. Right now, with the end of Buddy's life, he knew he would always play the guitar, good bad or indifferent, didn't matter, he would play it as a thankyou to this man who had died.

'Such dedication.' said Lionel.

'Why not? Do you think other people do that sort of thing, find that someone did something that they liked so much they started to do it themselves?'

'You mean are other people influenced by other people? Of course they are, read any biography and you find people admiring others and following in their footsteps, that's what drives civilisation forward. Without that we would just stagnate; go nowhere.'

'So be guided by Buddy Holly...' Sam thought for a while, 'Bit ordinary that, don't you reckon?'

'You could do worse. The bloke did well for himself, obviously pushed himself forward and achieved fame. You could do that if you had drive enough. At the very least you could play that box well enough to inspire someone else to do the same. Make some bird's heart beat a little faster, make some bloke buy a guitar and learn how to play it. At least you would have done something.'

'Yeh...' Sam imagined standing on stage playing, girls out front dancing to his rhythm. All he had to do was to find the missing chord in Peggy Sue. That elusive middle bit that was not E A or B bloody seven.

Hut building continued. Geordie Thompson found Sam.
'You're not going to hit me again?' Sam backed off
Geordie grinned his wide, white grin. 'Nah, once is enough and I'm sorry about that. You just got me a a bad bit.' Sam accepted the apology and felt that mention of Annabel would be best left unsaid.

Tedium

Robbie notched four notches into the flat grey three core cable. Sam took the end and began the tedious business of threading it through the wall top beams so that it ran the length of the hut. Once pulled the length they started back looping it down to each of the socket points. It seemed they had done this for months. Robbie whistled a tune. Sam joined in, the two men working in harmony as well as whistling the same tune.

'How many miles of this stuff have we laid?' Sam asked. Robbie reckoned he was obsessed by statistics.

'Millions mate, fucking millions.' He carried on the tune leaving Sam to ponder the millions. He supposed that he could actually work it out given that he had signed for all the cables. Drum lengths were on there. Maybe he would suggest that to Sam and let him do the working out.

'You could look up the cable invoices,' he said then continued to whistle the tune.

'Bugger that,' thought Sam.

They worked on in silence. The sun beat down outside and the wind curled about the part finished huts. The wood smelled of pine, a new scent for the otherwise scentless island. Scentless if you didn't count the diesel and the ciggy smoke and the cooking from the mess hall.

'There were no butterflies'. The thought suddenly struck Sam. Moths but no butterflies. No jungle he supposed just the rows of palm trees, all seventy thousand of them. Not real jungle, not the sort of stuff you had to hack your way through. Robbie interrupted his train of thought.

'How'dya get on with Geordie? Saw him chatting to you back there.'

'OK. He said he was sorry, some trouble back home, his bird knocking around with some other bloke. I reckon I took the punch for the other bloke.' Sam carried on with pulling and looping.

'Anyway he's going to treat me to the pictures so can't be that bad, can it?'

'You know you'll have to sit down the front don't you? I don't know whether it's his eyes or whether he's just tight and will only pay a shilling. You'll be down the front with him and Yorkie Carr. Stiff neck mate.'

They sat in the second row. Yorkie Carr leaned back and stared at the big screen with satisfaction. He took a swig from his first can.

'Why are you down in the front with us?' he asked.

'Being paid for. I'm broke and Geordie could only lend be a bob. Screen's big from here.' Sam leaned back on the tubular chair digging the back tube into the sand. The cartoon started unbelievably distorted from this angle.

Sam got the fact about butterflies in a day or two later. A discussion in the cookhouse.

'I've seen a butterfly, ' Sid said.

'Where?' asked Sam as if the location would enable a check to be made.

'In the trees.'

'It'll have been a moth.' Tommy Marks said with authority. 'No butterflies out here, know why?' he threw the question in. They all shook their heads and waited for the scientific explanation.

'No fucking cabbages! Obvious, aint it.'

They had spent eleven months on the island, watched bombs being tested, had built everything from roads to huts with sewage systems in between. Sam detected that most of them felt tired. The island was permanent army, there was no civvy street out here, no walking down a paved road with girls to chat up and cinema's to choose from. The whole gang felt weary of the constant sun and sea. At the end of February the first sign of the end of the tour came with the removal of their battle dress uniforms from the stores. Shaken clean and hung up in their lockers the brown uniforms looked tired and uncomfortable.

Rumours began to circulate based on the year being completed but finally March sixteenth was earmarked for the day of their return to England.

'What you going to do when we get home, then? Scouse wondered.

'Go on leave; we get four weeks don't we?' Sam began to contemplate four weeks at home with Grace. He had never really got on with his step mother. They had a slightly different point of view that made agreement always just off centre, or that was how it felt to Sam. Grace was kind, not spiteful or bad tempered, in fact as he thought about her he realised that he was very lucky to have a firm and reliable step mother to look after him. All the same he wondered what four weeks at home would be like.

Leave had always been a problem. He had never found any enjoyment, no big enjoyment that was, in being at home other than the fact that he was away from the constant discipline of the army. If he could have gone on leave, in London that is, with his mates from the army that would have been fine but he left them behind. Somehow he had never managed to be in touch with his secondary school mates. Adams, Robinson and Wellsy had been left behind when he left Hillbrook and went to the Brixton School of building. Doc Shaw had then been his best friend - not a good choice when he considered it was Doc's influence that had landed him in the army. Doc had slipped from view thus leaving a fairly lonely time at Gassiot road.

There was Pam Williams the daughter of the fish and chip shop man. Black hair and big eyes, beautiful. Not much hope there; she had told him to piss off once so he reckoned that Gassiot road would be unproductive.

Christmas leave was the longest at three weeks and that went past pretty quickly with all the celebrations. Summer leave was shorter with maybe a trip to the seaside. When Dad had died Sam had acted the man going with Grace on a holiday to Margate. Blazer and flannels had been the style of the thing and they had walked by the sea talking. Dad's absence had loomed large and Sam had so little conversation that the whole thing had become memorable for its blankness. Four weeks home in March. He wondered how cold the weather and the atmosphere would be in Tooting.

CHAPTER 22

Eighteenth March nineteen fifty nine.

Came the day.

Wednesday on Christmas Island. Kit packed and sent to the airfield in a truck. Early breakfast the last in the high windblown circus tent of the cookhouse. Dressed now in battle dress khaki, shirt sleeve order but carrying BD jacket and great coat ready for the trip. Hawaii, Vancouver with an overnight stop then on to Gander and finally home to Stansted.

'Bloody hot in this lot. Hope we take off on time. Remember coming out in this kit?' Sid grinned, 'you were sick.'

'Only nearly.' Sam remembered and determined to give his orange to Sid. 'It was a bit different then, we weren't acclimatised. You can have my orange. It was that that did it.'

The year suddenly seemed to have been no time at all. The 'days to do' charts had become meaningless as the date became known and the time ceased to be endless but became finite. This time next week became the subject.

Sam began to think benevolent thoughts about the place, began to soften the experience. They'd had some good times; seen hydrogen bombs go off, sailed and got pissed under the sun and the stars. Sweated and ached and enjoyed cheap fags for a year. He'd caught an octopus.

The trucks pulled up outside and they collected their sandwiches from the counter. Sam gave his orange to Sid, shouldered his guitar and hoisted himself aboard. They went back along the road they had arrived on. This time black tarmac not dusty rolled coral.

There was the RAF Hastings, silver and white in the early morning light. Sam remembered arrival day, the airsick feeling, the heat - even in the heavy battle dress the acclimatisation made that initial heat difficult to recall. They waited at the edge of the white concrete runway smoking, almost chain smoking! getting ready for the six hour fag free journey. At last the order to board was given and they filed out to the plane. Sam wished he wasn't so worried about being sick. He concentrated on walking and then put his foot on the step and lifted himself up and away from the ground of Christmas island. He looked round as he climbed. 'Roll on home,' he thought and ducked through the doorway to find a seat next to a window.

By the window? What was he going to see?

'Why sit by the window?' Sid asked as if reading his mind. Sid always sat in the gangway seat to stretch his legs.

'Used to sit by the window when we went up to Scotland in the Flying Scotsman. Once I'd got over being sick I would watch the telephone wires going up and down: where they hung between the poles, lowest point and then up to the cross bars again. It was soothing.'

'Just sea this time.' Sid pushed his legs out as the door closed and the flight sergeant began his talk about not smoking in the bogs. The engines roared and the plane taxied to the end of the white runway.

'Don't let us crash,' prayed Sam as the seat pressed into his back and the ground flew faster and faster past his window and then they lifted away from the white strip. The perspective dipped away showing the rows of palms and the road and then sea. In six hours time he would be nearer to Loretta. He felt the sob fresh in his throat.

Hickam Field again

Eighteenth March nineteen fifty nine. Tuesday in Honolulu. Something to do with the date line. Hickam field spread beneath them. The buildings, looking like some toy town models, growing larger and larger, then speeding past the window and finally the bump and the changing engine note, then taxiing to a standstill.

'Don't leave nothing behind, it'll only get chucked,' the flight sergeant ushered them off.

'Wouldn't fancy his job,' Sid lit a cigarette at the earliest opportunity, 'must be a non smoker. Figure it; six hours here, six hours back and eight hours kip that's four hours smoking left. Might as well give up.'

'You came here on leave,' Sam halted the mathematics, 'what did you get up to?'

Sid drew deeply on his cigarette. 'Same as you; drank a lot. Didn't meet any decent birds like you did. Mind you, reckon that was a good thing looking at the state of you when you came back.'

Sam pondered a life without commitment. Don't go after girls, keep your heart intact. Nah. He decided he would rather have met Loretta and had the broken heart. The warm Hawaiian air seemed to carry the perfume she wore. He began to look about as if certain she would appear. 'Silly sod!' he told himself, 'Loretta was in Washington teaching little American kids how to read, lucky little buggers. In Miss Leicher's class. Golden hair. He went further back and thought of Miss Curtis at his primary school in Undine street, Tooting. She wore a red sweater that showed off her figure; her hair a copy of Veronica Lake's with the front curl hiding her eye. How old had he been then? Ten?

They were herded onto a bus and taken over to the mess hall for a mid afternoon meal. It was still as Sam remembered although fairly empty at this time of day. The pancakes were still on offer and Sam decided that they would be the least sick making things you could have. Lionel told them that they had dropped back a day. It was Tuesday.

'Wonder if Jackie Bones had sent his football coupon in?' Lionel remembered the long discussion about knowing the results.

Two hours later they walked across to the smartest aircraft they had ever seen.

'Bristol Britannia,' Lionel announced. 'The whispering giant. The Yanks are really jealous about it. Lands and takes off in less distance than anything comparable they've got.'

'BOAC written on the side, that'll mean we can smoke.' Tommy Marks cheered up.

'And hostesses, look.' Lionel pointed. Four airhostesses accompanied what Sam presumed to be the pilots. Smart in white blouses and navy blue pencil skirts. Neat little hats. 'The world is suddenly full of women...' he thought.

Travelling

Take off and Sam sat watching the islands pass beneath; a view Loretta would have seen on her 'airplane outing' as she had called it. He supposed that flying to Vancouver would at least be heading in the right direction to be nearer to her but then immediately realised that he would eventually be flying away from her once more.

Was Vancouver warm at this time of year? Should he stop thinking about Loretta? Start thinking about Jean? There was no magic about Jean; she was a pen friend with the accent on friend. It was not her fault, how could it be? They had never touched, never stood close to one another, never felt the warmth of closeness. He remembered Loretta once more and looked out of the window at the blue Pacific.

'Beats the Hastings dunit?' Sid stretched his legs. There was enough room under the seat in front to be able to do this without blocking the aisle.

The airhostess approached. He beckoned her 'Scuse me miss, do you know if we will be on this plane all the way back to England?'

'I hope so, I'm heading for some leave in London so you've got this plane and us girls all the way home, that's why you get a night in Vancouver you lucky lads.'

'What about money? A night out is no good without some cash.'

'Shouldn't worry too much, you can change some at the airport to tide you over but if your short most hotels take sterling. Big tourist industry so can't afford to be fussy. Excuse me.'

She moved on to attend to another 'customer'. Sam thought it must be funny for her to be shepherding a bunch of squaddies in khaki uniforms rather than rich civilians. In every seat a brown clad, deeply tanned soldier. The plane droned on. A meal was served and beer offered. Sam's mind drifted back and forth from the island to home.

Vancouver

Vancouver was wet and cold. Sam hauled his greatcoat on, donned his beret and made a run with the rest of the lads for the bus. Then he remembered he'd left his guitar on the parcel shelf.

'Shit!'

'What's wrong mate?' Scouse settled beside him on the coach seat.

'I've left my guitar on the plane,'

'No worries, we're on the same plane to Gander, no one 'll pinch that battered old thing. Be there when we get back on in the morning. No worries.'

Sam remembered the hostess telling Sid that. He settled back in the seat as the coach swung out of the airport. This was the way to travel, no passports, no customs. No guitar. It seemed strange to be without it. He had hauled it halfway round the world and should have been careful enough to haul it back again but no, in his half dozy state he had only worried about being sick. Forgotten his friend and left it on the luggage rack.

They arrived at the hotel Sylvia. A sky scraper! It seemed so modern, so out of the pictures. London by contrast was still in that battered post war state, like a boxer bloodied and bruised; elated at having won the fight but not yet properly cleaned up, the scars from the fight very visible. He paired off with Robbie and they took the lift to the seventh floor. Not at the top but still high enough to make looking out of the window a bit dizzying.

They met up again in the bar.

'My aunt got bombed out during the war,' Tommy Marks sipped his beer. The conversation had started with Sam saying how tidy and modern Vancouver looked compared with London.

'What happens when your house gets bombed then?' Sid wondered.

'Well, aunt Nell moved in with us; still lives with us to this day.'

'What about all her belongings, furniture and things?'

'Match wood. V2 hit the place while she was down the shop. Came home and didn't have a larder to put the food in so she walked round to our house and that was it.'

'Bloody hell,' Sid scratched his head, 'I suppose we were lucky in Didcot, Germans couldn't find the place let alone bomb it.'

'I knew a bloke in Southampton,' Terry Ogilvy joined in and Sam reckoned the Bargate would get a mention any time soon, 'going to work one morning and getting stopped by a policeman. Wanted to know where he was going. 'Work' said Les - that was his name - 'Where 'bouts?' the policeman wanted to know. 'Down Hanover buildings, by the Bargate' - Sam smiled and decided that he must see this object one day - 'Can't go down there' the policeman told him, 'unexploded thousand pounder down there and Hanover buildings is flat as a pan cake;

rubble.' Les had tramped off back home and wondered where the next pay packet was coming from.'

The conversation made Sam think that his mum, his real mum, must have lived in constant fear of being 'bombed out'. With Dad away at the war and her at home with him just a toddler... she must have been very brave. Sam wished he could remember more of her than just the dressing gown sleeve and the fact that she always seemed to know he was picking his nose underneath the blankets in the dark tent of bedclothes behind her back while the distant thumps of an air raid provided a sound track.

He slept like a log in the real hotel bed.

Next morning breakfast in the vast dining room of the hotel Sylvia was the same miracle that had happened in Hawaii; food in abundance and self service. Pan cakes with maple syrup had to be eaten.

'We're in Canada so you have to show willing and eat their food, only right really.' Scouse said.

'Would they get scouse in Liverpool?' Sam wondered.

'Too right. Probably love it. Put hairs on their chest.' Scouse loaded more pancakes onto his plate and dribbled maple syrup over them.

'Coach at ten,' sergeant Chant announced, 'no hanging about. Anyone missing it will be left behind,' a little cheer went up, 'and have to pay his own fare home on the next plane,' a little groan went up.

'You could miss it and nip over to Washington, see that bird your always on about.' Scouse was being his usual ingenious self.

'Good idea mate, got any money?'

Scouse admitted that would be a problem.

Opposite the hotel was a lake; English beach the receptionist told Sam. He and Scouse headed out into the cold fresh morning. Everything smelt different. The car fumes had an almost antiseptic edge to their scent, totally unlike the fumes in Hawaii or on the island. Cigarettes tasted different.

'Do you think things will smell and taste like this when we get home?'

'Everything tastes and smells better in Liverpool,' Scouse dragged on his ciggy, 'I don't care how it smells, it's home. Four weeks with nothing to do but eat me mams cooking and sleep in my own bed. I 'spect you feel the same about London, yeh?'

'I suppose.' Sam envied the Liverpudlean's stable home life. He would get home to Grace and her rules. No Dad to back him up or pour oil on troubled waters. The sun broke through the clouds making the wet grass sparkle.

'Quarter to ten. Time to get back. Where's next?'

'Gander,' Scouse stubbed his fag out, 'where ever the fuck that is.

Onward, ever onward

The plane was the same and Sam's guitar still perched on the luggage rack. Belted in Sam felt the pre take off anxiety then became enthralled as Vancouver spread out beneath them.

Canada is made of trees and lakes. Six hours of trees and lakes. The only relief being that the land gradually whitened with snow the further north and east they flew. The hostess told them that it would be eight in the evening when they arrived. Sam looked at his watch but being still on island time it made no sense. The light began to fade and Sam slept.

Gander was cold, very cold. Even with his greatcoat on and the collar turned up, Sam felt the piercing cold; a cold he had not felt since he was a child. Scotland maybe? He was too cold to remember. He clenched his teeth and marched toward the low buildings. Once through the door he and the others found themselves in a broad, brightly lit corridor. An Eskimo came in tramping snow from big fur boots. Sam watched in amazement as the hooded fur jacket was removed to reveal the head of an air hostess. The fur trousers were pushed down and she stepped from the mass that included the boots. From a bag she produced a hat and a pair of shoes and finally resolved into a slim hostess.

'Bloody hell!' Scouse said waking Sam to the real world once more.

Gander was quite warm once in the building. Doors lead to a vast area. The corridor had been a sort of air lock or heat lock.

'Scot of the Antarctic up here. Way down below freezing out there. I wouldn't want to live in a place like this.'

'Bit like Didcot a couple of winters back.' Sid joined them clutching a drink and a hamburger. 'Went skating on the ponds for weeks.'

'But this is the middle of March.'

'You are not wrong. I think I'd prefer Didcot.'

The three hour wait passed quickly. There were shops and a bar so they wanted for nothing. Most of all there were women. After a year of male company it took Sam a bit of time to get back into seeing a woman without staring.

Out into the cold and a long wait on the 'plane steps, then the warm familiar seat and the take off. The pilot told them it was eleven o'clock. Acceleration; Sam felt a little more confident.

'Becoming seasoned travellers, ' said Sid, reading his mind again.

CHAPTER 23

Home again

England

The pilot announced that the weather over southern England was dull with a temperature of forty four and that it would rain later. The flight from Gander had been mostly in the dark. Sid had woken Sam to watch the dawn coming up as they flew further east. Then clear sky and the first sight of proper country with fields and hedges. Not desert, not jungle or endless woods and lakes but fields which would turn yellow in the summer sun. England.

'Thank you!' said Sam, 'rain and cold, just what I needed!'

The pilot hoped they had enjoyed their flight and the hostesses started making sure their seats were upright. They descended to Stansted, a sprawl of low buildings in the middle of nowhere.

'Where's Stansted?' Geordie asked.

'Here, England,' Sam had no idea where the place was and concentrated on dealing with the sinking feeling in the pit of his stomach. 'Ten more minutes,' he told himself then they would be on the ground and he wouldn't be worried about feeling sick.

Stansted, where ever it was, did not look too much like an international airport and as usual they had to walk from the plane over to the flimsy looking buildings. Once there the usual wait ensued. Then the RAF coach turned up. With the luggage going by truck Sam had only his guitar to contend with.

'Should have left that battered old thing behind, mate,' Sid slid it into the overhead rack and sat down. The journey began and Sam stared out of the window at the cold, almost bleak countryside. When they went through villages it seemed the locals all looked rosy cheeked.

'Been out in the sun,' was Sid's opinion.

'Freezin' bloody cold, more like,' Sam felt chilly even in the comparative warmth of the coach. What a long time ago it seemed since he had got off the plane on Christmas Island and sweated buckets, all the time feeling sick. Now he was back home in the cold, wet greyness that was England in March. At least he didn't feel sick this time.

The coach found London and they began to weave through the east end and finally turned into a vast concrete yard, a TA depot, with what looked like a hanger at its end. The coach parked beneath the canopy, out of the rain and they trooped in, cold and tired. The usual tables were laid out and they stepped forward for the disembarkation ritual. Leave pass:

four weeks. Travel warrant. Leave pay. They sat and smoked, waiting while they all got processed.

Sergeant Chant called them to attention.

'Lucky lads,' he started, 'the coach will take you and your luggage to Waterloo station and drop you off there, unless, that is, any of you want to go from here, godforsaken place that it is' He looked about and found Tommy Marks who nodded that it was his home ground.

'You've all been seen to. Four weeks leave and then back to Barton Stacey.' a murmur told him that nobody had any idea where Barton Stacey was. 'OK! OK! In the envelope with your travel warrant you will find instructions. Train to Andover and then a bus as far as I remember. Enjoy your leave and behave yourselves. No getting the first bird you meet up the duff!'

And so the Christmas Island adventure was over. Sam wondered if anyone would say thank you for the roads and the sewage system and the lovely wooden huts. But then he wondered who the someone would be. Just a job really. You're in the Engineers so that is what you do. He hauled his kit bag and guitar onto the coach and watched the world go by. It began to rain, just like the pilot had said.

Home

The tube from Waterloo was the northern line. The longest tunnel in the world Dad had said. Seventeen and a quarter miles long and Tooting Broadway was on it, forth one from the end. London heaved about him once more as he lugged his heavy kit bag about. His guitar, slung across his shoulders, sounded now and again as he walked. Familiar ground, back to playing truant - where was Loretta? He heard her saying 'Hooky' and saw her lovely smile - back to going up London with doc Shaw but this time in uniform wearing boots and beret. The boots sounded against the rounded walls and he felt the whoosh of warm air that signified the movement of trains somewhere. The smell was stale; people, wet coats and cigarette smoke.

Tooting Broadway arrived and he rode the escalator up and walked the wide hall to the pavement. Home. The curve of the station entrance the only thing exotic in the rainy greyness of the main road.

'Cut through the market as it's raining,' he thought. Cheap Jack was still there and he almost stopped where his Father had stood. Egge marked the exit. A misspelling from the barrow boy's past that had stuck. Over Totterdown road, past the Bagwash, and up Blakenham road to Gassiot, the road lined by plane trees with their smooth bark coming away in flakes. And then he was there. He knocked the door. No answer. He walked around the corner to Mr Marshall's shop.

Mr Marshall lived in the downstairs flat of number one hundred with Mrs Cullan and owned the shop round the corner in Franciscan road making belts and buckles for ladies dresses. He would have a key. The shop smelled of rubber solution. The buckles were metal and the material was stuck on. At one time Dad and Grace had made them at home to raise a bit of extra money. Sam remembered the glue - Charlie decanted it into dried milk tins for home use - it was good for lighting the fire but you had to be sparing. The fumes from the empty tins could be sniffed giving a weird sensation of being able to feel your teeth!

'You're home John,' Charlie's grin widened as he reached out and took Sam's free hand shaking it firmly, 'didn't get blown up by no atomic bombs then!'

'No, they all missed.'

Charlie Marshall, bluff and red faced with thick, iron grey hair, laughed. Charlie's accent was clipped; Jewish if there was such an accent.

'Key', he pulled out a spare, 'Pop it down to Cicely when you're in. She's out with Barbara at the moment. Be back later. You look brown as a nut. Been out in the sun, ha ha!'

'I'll tell you all about it soon,' Sam promised, 'tired at the moment and I need to warm up.'

'Hot bath and a cup of tea, that's the remedy for chill when returning from the tropics. You get on John.'

It was funny being called by his proper name once more, it meant he was really home, back in civvy street for a month. Ordinary clothes, no first parades. Sleeping in a room by himself; silent and dark with none of the little noises that twenty odd other blokes made. He let himself in and struggled up the stairs to the flat. It was half past three in the afternoon.

Time for a bath. The gas geyser popped into life. Sam put a kettle on the gas and felt the tiny kitchen begin to warm. He wondered whether it was an unusually cold day. He was freezing. The geyser would not be hurried. He found the tea pot and brewed the tea while he waited.

The flat was dull. Never particularly bright, even in the sunniest of weather, only the room at the front had big enough windows to render it light. The layout of the flat was odd. Being built on a hill the house was at ground level in the front. You could go downstairs to Mrs Cullan's flat, once there you could walk out of the back door into the garden! Same as the convent. Sam wondered if he should light a fire? The bath was ready and he lowered himself into the very hot water putting his tea cup on the floor. He lay back feeling the heat soak into his body.

Silence

There was no sound. Nothing save the swish of his own blood circulating. No mates, no flapping canvas; alone and silent. He let his eyes drift around the room. The pale green walls the same as ever. The round mark in the plaster by the toilet, a reminder of the sink plunger 'tomahawk' incident. The frosted window casting an almost grey light into the room. He realised that he lay where his father's bicycle had stood. In the bath with its front wheel between the taps. He remembered sitting on the closed toilet seat, which he had French polished, while Dad put his wet gear on prior to cycling to work.

'Do you know why I am putting this on?' Dad would ask.

'To keep you dry.' Sam would say.

'A ha!' Dad would laugh, 'to keep other people dry. If I put this lot on,' he would say pulling up the plastic trousers, 'it will not rain. Leave it off and it will rain sure as eggs is eggs. I'm a philanthropist, looking after my fellow man,' and with that he would heave the heavy black bicycle out of the bath, haul it onto his shoulder and make his way carefully down the stairs. Big, solid, dependable Dad. Sam shifted in the water and wished Dad was still here.

'Oh bollocks!' he said the words out loud as he realised the only towel he had in the room was the little hand towel that hung from below the wash basin. He pulled the plug and stood up drying himself quickly before the heat of the bath wore off.

The rest of the afternoon was spent finding clothes. Vests he had never warn but now he searched in the closets for anything which would keep the March wind out. He found a vest. Had it been his father's? He found an overcoat which he had forgotten, shoes and winter socks. He dressed himself with as many as he could wear. He wondered again should he light the fire but then decided that he would walk down and meet Grace from work. In his school days he had done this, standing outside the railings by the main gate of St Georges hospital where his stepmother had been in charge of the linen department. He would lean against the railings watching as people came and went into the vast hospital. Grace would come out sometimes happy, sometimes angry...

'I'll give her soul mate!' she had cursed one day when Miss Kopp had suggested that they were so alike as to be such a thing. He wondered what the effect would be today. When he had written he had not known the exact dates of the homeward journey; she knew he would be home mid March. That had seemed good enough.

She smiled. 'Home then?'

'Home.'

'We had better have a celebration then. What would you like for your tea?'

'Sausage and mash.' Sam had no hesitation. Not pancakes with maple syrup nor ham and peaches. Hash browns and crisp bacon. It was nice to be ordinary again, sausages, mash and peas with a thick gravy made with onions.

'I'll get some sausages in the market. What was the journey like?'

'Long and boring really. There wasn't much to see. The Pacific ocean is deserted, Canada is trees and lakes and we came over the Atlantic in the dark. We landed at Stansted.'

'Where's that?' Grace took his arm as they crossed the road.

'North of London is all I know. The coach came in through the east end.'

And so Sam, now John again for four weeks, walked back to the flat with his stepmother Grace. She now an isolated figure since her husband's death and he also an isolated figure since coming home. No warm 'me mam,' like Scouse, no extended family like Tommy, no sense of place like Sid. He felt nearest to Robbie but without the comfort of alcohol. It would be four weeks before he would see any of them again.

When they got home he had lit the fire. Grace had cooked the sausages and mash. The meal had been a lovely welcome back to the ordinary. The wireless had muttered in the background and Grace had sat at her sewing machine.

'Been writing to a pen friend in Southampton,' he told her.

'Girl ?'

'Yes. Jean.'

'Be careful,' standard advice of the day.

The next morning Sam set off to find Southampton and the Bargate.

As Remembered.

Epilogue

Sam caught a train to Southampton and arrived there at about eight on a very sunny morning. He walked up the hill toward the white clock tower (The Civic Centre) and found a vast open space with a rose garden its main feature. He walked on and eventually found Sainsbury's in the high street and finally came face to face with The Bargate. He met Jean, stayed at her parents' house for a week then went home to London once more.

But, even that is not the end of the story. The main end is that eventually he and Robbie discovered Southampton as an excellent weekend venue for women and, in Robbie's case, booze. They would travel down from Barton Stacey on Saturday and stay in a B&B in Ordnance Road and socialise in a city filled with women. Sam met his future wife, married her and lived in Southampton for the next twenty seven years. He and she had a son, David and Sam settled to a steady job with the Southern Electricity Board.

John Smart. October 2015.

To Ian Smith, a friend connected by my guitar ambitions described within, who drummed us to success in THE HELLIONS!

John Smart.

16547108R00106

Printed in Great Britain
by Amazon